WARRIORS IN PEACETIME

WARRIORS
IN
PEACETIME

THE MILITARY AND DEMOCRACY
IN LATIN AMERICA
NEW DIRECTIONS FOR US POLICY

Edited by
GABRIEL MARCELLA

FRANK CASS

First published 1994 in Great Britain by
FRANK CASS & CO. LTD
2 Park Square, Milton Park,
Abingdon, Oxon, OX14 4RN

and in the United States of America by
FRANK CASS
c/o International Specialized Book Services, Inc.,
270 Madison Ave,
New York NY 10016

Transferred to Digital Printing 2005

British Library Cataloguing in Publication Data

Warriors in Peacetime:Military and
Democracy in Latin America – New
Directions for US Policy. – (Special
Issue of the Journal "Small Wars &
Insurgencies" Series, ISSN 0959–2318)
I. Marcella, Gabriel II. Series
327.7308

ISBN 0–7146–4585–0
ISBN 0–7146–4115–4

Library of Congress Cataloging-in-Publication Data

Warriors in peacetime : the military and democracy in Latin America,
new directions for US policy / edited by Gabriel Marcella.
  p.   cm.
"Studies first appeared in a special issue on 'Warriors in
Peacetime' of Small Wars & Insurgencies, vol. 4, no. 3 (Winter
1993)"--T.p. verso.
Includes bibliographical references
ISBN 0–7146–4585–0 : -- ISBN 0–7146–4115–4 (pbk.) :
1. Latin America--Armed Forces. 2. Civil–military relations-
-Latin America. 3. Democracy--Latin America. 4. United States-
-Military policy. I. Marcella, Gabriel.
UA602.3.W37   1994
355'.03308--dc20   94–1380
                                                              CIP

This group of studies first appeared in a Special Issue on 'Warriors in Peacetime'
of *Small Wars & Insurgencies*, Vol.4, No. 3 (Winter 1993), published by Frank
Cass & Co. Ltd.

Typeset by Photoprint

*Cover artwork depicts the Flag of the [Hispanic]
Race flown throughout Latin America on
12 October each year.*

Contents

Foreword

The papers collected in this volume are the product of the Warriors in Peacetime Conference held at the Inter-American Defense College, Washington, DC, on 11–12 December 1992. Special thanks are due to General James Harding of the College for hosting the conference, and the Strategic Outreach Programme, US Army War College, for providing financial support. This meeting was organised to explore the relationship between the theory and practice of democracy in Latin America, on the one hand, and the changing roles of the US and Latin American militaries, on the other. The dialogue brought together a diverse group of scholars and civilian and military officials from the United States and Latin America. It was constructed around three major addresses, one by Ambassador Luigi Einaudi, US Permanent Representative to the Organization of American States, the second by General George Joulwan, Commander-in-Chief of the US Southern Command, and the final by the Honorable Bernard Aronson, Assistant Secretary of State for Inter-American Affairs. Ambassador Einaudi has been throughout his academic and government career an intellectual catalyst for the serious study of the Latin American military and democracy. Three panels addressed the themes: 'The New World Order and the Democratic Imperative in Civil-Military Relations', 'The Unfinished Business of Security', and 'Winning the Peace'.

The question of what military warriors should do in peacetime is especially timely not only in Latin America but throughout the world. Some Latin American countries continue to be threatened by guerrilla movements, or narcotrafficking, or even the possibility of the delegitimation of democracy, with consequences that can only be dimly perceived. Military institutions across the globe must rethink their utility to the societies they serve. They must also adapt their strategies to the radically changed geopolitical environment. This rethinking has reached advanced levels in Latin America. It was therefore remarkable to observe the intense and frank interaction during the conference among distinguished experts from the academic, government, and military communities of the United States and Latin America. The conference reaffirmed some fundamental lessons that are of direct utility to policymakers: substantive communication between civilians and military is fundamental for national security, democracy and human rights must be nurtured jointly by civilian and military authorities especially as they deal with internal war and international criminal enterprises in the form of narcotraffickers, and civilian responsibility in military affairs is also fundamental to democratic order.

US policymakers need to sustain a strategy of constructive engagement with the Latin American military institutions for the purpose of strengthening the foundations of democracy. Such a strategy will, however, not succeed unless civilian professional competence in all of the interrelated issues raised din this volume – military strategy, planning and operations, intelligence, roles and missions, human rights, low-intensity conflict, civil-military relations – is strengthened. Therefore, engaging and educating Latin American civilians in these areas is the new compelling challenge for the policy of the United States and the democratic community of nations.

GENERAL (RETD.) FRED F. WOERNER
Boston University

Warriors in Peacetime: Future Missions of the Latin American Armed Forces

GABRIEL MARCELLA

The Army is in reasonably good condition, considering the fact that peace and politics are always more damaging than war.
General William T. Sherman, US Army, 1883

When the armed forces don't have a purpose within a military strategy, there will be no lack of political and economic groups disposed to take them to purposes which do not correspond to their nature, to their organisation, and to their training.
General Humberto de Alencar Castelo Branco,
Army of Brazil, 1957

There can be no expression of a desire to return to political power when experience tells us that the result is totally negative for our country and fundamentally so for the armed forces.
General Hector Rios Ereñu, Army of Argentina, 1986

But the real threat we now face is the threat of the unknown, the uncertain.
General Colin L. Powell, Chairman, US Joint Chiefs of Staff, 1992

The reflections of Generals Sherman, Castelo Branco, Rios Ereñu, and of General Colin L. Powell are compelling reminders of the challenges that all military institutions face during peacetime. They must maintain their professionalism, avoid partisan politics, and be ready to fight, just in case. As we enter the New World Order we may face a similar challenge. We may also be on the threshold of a new golden age of strategy. Just as the immediate post-World War II was one of strategic vision and creativity by statesmen, we now have the opportunity to think through and shape a democratic international order that puts an end to aggressive warfare.

This essay explores the universal question of what should warriors do after the hot peace of the cold war. It will specifically deal with Latin American military warriors and how the United States should engage its policy. The author is mindful of the risks of a foreigner articulating views on an issue that is so central to the sovereign civil-military dialogue in Latin American countries. Yet, the dialogue is international and multi-dimensional. We have much to learn from each other's national experiences in order to pursue the common objectives of peace, democracy, and economic development. The purpose, therefore, is to engender further dialogue and scholarly reflection so that common efforts break down barriers to communication and bear fruit across borders and institutions.

Power, Political Purpose, and Military Sufficiency in Modern Strategy

The military professional's responsibility is to be prepared to apply violence in a measured, ethical and legal manner for national political purpose. This admonition is not advocacy of war, but recognition of the reality of conflict. In this century the world has moved toward the abolition of aggressive warfare by the United Nations Charter. Nonetheless, the Iraqi invasion of Kuwait in 1990 and the smouldering sub-national conflicts speak to the endurance of war and to the responsibility of the international community to deal with it. This leads us to a simple but profound conclusion: though efforts should continue to prevent war, there will probably be war. The military strategist Admiral J.C. Wylie addressed this conundrum in the context of US civil-military relations:

> The assumption that there will be war is in no sense a desire of war for war's sake. But the necessity for the military man to assume that there will be war is something that consistently and subtly irritates the civilian. The civilian comes to feel that study or preparation for war must somehow be advocacy of war, although the cancer specialist never runs the risk of being viewed as advocating cancer. There is really a sort of aura effect – war is brutal, inhuman, and cruel, and one must be the same if one discusses it.[1]

The lexicon of the military is power, its utility and dis-utility for political purpose. Power is the ability to influence the behaviour of other nations in the international system in order to advance a nation's interests. Those interests are reducible to the core: defence of homeland, economic well-being, international order, preserving a nation's values, and protecting the environment.[2] The competitive international system requires each nation to maximise its power in order to advance the well-being of its citizens.

The components of national power are the aggregate of social, intellectual, economic, political, technological, and military capabilities. Joseph Nye of Harvard University speaks of hard and soft power.[3] The latter refers to the attractiveness of a society's values as well as its capacity to adjust to the competitive international system. In the absence of a functioning and equitable international system of collective security, the nation-state reserves the right to resort to the military deterrent in order to defend its core interests.

Military power is a discrete component of national power. It is not absolute, however. It is dynamic, situational, and relative to the physical, geopolitical, and political circumstances, and to the opponent capabilities and intentions. The components of military power are both quantitative and qualitative:

Quantitative	*Qualitative*
1. Force size and structure	1. Strategic and tactical doctrines
2. Weapons systems	2. Training and readiness
3. Mobility	3. Morale
4. Logistics	4. Military leadership, command and control
5. Industry and technology	5. National will and societal cohesion
6. Strategic reach and sustainability	6. Alliances
	7. National leadership and nature of political process

This mere listing tells us nothing about what is sufficient military power – specific forces and the strategy to employ to achieve the political purpose in given contigencies. Moreover, the utility of military power in a violent way is constrained in the modern world. International law and the abolition of aggressive war by Article 2 of the United Nations Charter is a constraint. Another is the very lethality of modern weapons technology, whether conventional or nuclear. Modern democratic political culture is also a constraint on warmaking. The Weinberger Doctrine, enunciated in 1984 by Secretary of Defense Caspar W. Weinberger, exemplifies this by counselling that the United States resort to force only under the following six conditions:[4]

1. That the issue be vital to the national interest.
2. That there be a clear intention of winning.
3. That there be clearly defined political and military objectives.
4. That there be a continual reassessment of the relationship between the political objectives and the forces employed, and adjust if necessary.
5. That the effort have the support of the American people and Congress.
6. That it be the last resort when diplomatic measures have failed.

The rigorous Weinberger Doctrine integrates the hard lessons learned by Americans in using force. It speaks of a social contract between the people, the government, and the military – a version of Clausewitz's remarkable trinity. The Doctrine is also a domestic political version of the ageless just war theory, which argues for a just cause and just means in the resort to war.

The depolarisation of the world is forcing drastic changes in US military strategy. As we adjust to the New World Order, the macro strategy will have the following features: strategic deterrence, forward presence (instead of forward defense), crisis response, force reconstitution, collective security, arms control, and peacetime engagement.

The US military is developing the 'Base Force'. It will be 'capabilities' rather than threat oriented. This will be a radical departure for a military organised since the inception of the Cold War to meet the global Soviet threat.

Despite these changes, the theory and art of military strategy will not change.[5] Political ends are to be achieved through the measured application of military means.

Military Missions and the New World Order

The emergence of a new world order and the attendant calls for demilitarising international relations urge us to consider the future missions of armed forces. Missions are the *raison d'être* of military institutions. In a democratic system they must be credible to both the military professional and to the society served. They must be founded on functions for which the military is uniquely organised, equipped, and trained, and from which they can develop *esprit de corps* and high morale. They must also not unduly compete with the civilian sector of society for resources, employment, rewards, or political power.

Because military power is so awesome and potentially destructive one must recall Georges Clemenceau's stark admonition: 'Generals cannot be trusted with anything, not even with war.' (The more popular version: 'War is too important to be left to generals.') But civilians can also be irresponsible in their advocacy of the military instrument. Thus the need for prudent and effective civilian control and constant communication between civilians and military on the utility of force. Military power, available as a legitimate instrument of state power, must be employed as a last resort in resolving either domestic or international conflict. Such use ranges from support to law enforcement agencies, to nation-building, show of force, coercive diplomacy, to deterring and, if necessary, fighting wars against conventional and unconventional threats, and finally, to shaping the peace and reconstituting order after the fighting. Last, missions must respond to the legitimate requirements of a nation for defense against identified threats. For the military the external threat is the primary responsibility. Internal security is normally the responsibility of police forces, and only when such forces are unable to handle the problem should the military be called upon – and then with minimum force. In nearly all societies militaries provide a law enforcement reserve available as the last resort.

In nearly all societies the military also serves the collateral function of social integrator. By acquiring self-esteem, patriotism, discipline, and administrative and technical skills a soldier or officer becomes a more productive member of society upon reentry. By learning engineering, education, health, or communication, the military helps build societal capabilities. By developing leadership skills and responsible command over troops and subordinates, the military imparts to society such benefits as respect for the rule of law, respect for human rights, and civilian control over the organised means of violence.

The boundaries of relations between civilians and military are blurring. The revolution in communications and the international disorder brought on by terrorism, narcotrafficking, the clandestine movement of people and arms, the proliferation of weapons technologies, the persistence of subnational, ethnic and international conflict, the threat to ecological integrity, and the recurrence of natural disasters diminish the traditional distinctions between civilian and military jurisdictions. This calls for greater integration between civilian and military efforts. In addition, the end of East-West military competition provides new incentives for democratic societies to reduce the size of military establishments in order to allocate resources to economic development. It should also be an incentive to seek non-military solutions to international disputes. Indeed, rational calculations of the cost and lethality of modern weaponry render them so destructive as to demand a reappraisal of the strategy of limited war and the Clausewitzian notion of achieving the political objective through the instrument of force.

Moreover, the emergence of fledgling democracies in Eastern Europe and in the republics of the Commonwealth of Independent States requires new military institutions, subordinated not to the Communist Party but to government accountable to the people. This will also require a new military professionalism. The models for such professionalism are likely to be the United States and the NATO community.

These introductory comments are important because they deal with the language and values of a universal military culture. They also deal with the ongoing reappraisal of the conceptual underpinnings of defense policy and military strategy. Even Latin American militaries, which were distant from the principal theatres of the Cold War, need to take note. The societies they serve are demanding adjustment to new strategic realities.

The United States, Latin America, and the End of the Cold War: The Search for a New Strategic Relationship

The armed forces of the United States and Latin America are deeply affected by the end of the Cold War. The United States will reduce its military by 25 to 30 per cent in the next five years. There will be a significant, indeed radical, shift in its global strategy – from forward defense to forward presence. It will still rely on the spectrum of conventional and nuclear forces but will deemphasise the nuclear. US nuclear weapons will be reduced from 21,000 (13,000 strategic, 8,000 tactical) in 1990 to 5,100 (3,500 strategic, 1,600 tactical) by 2003. NATO will remain the centrepiece of its alliance structure. NATO's forces will be smaller and more flexible and will be prepared to deal with regional crises and contingencies rather than the old threat from the East. Arms control will be an integral part of military strategy and hopefully lead to denuclearisation and lower conventional force levels while building greater confidence in the emerging security environment.

The radical changes underway are stimulating an appropriate debate about how far American defence responsibilities should reach, especially given the calls for strengthening the domestic base of power. At the same time, the United Nations is emerging as a more effective element in international security and peacekeeping. In early 1993 the United Nations had 13 peacekeeping missions around the globe.

This reappraisal is taking place in all democracies. It carries with it the potential demise of the post-World War II strategic relationship with Latin America variously entitled hemispheric or inter-American security. This relationship entailed a panoply of military cooperation and security assistance programmes designed to provide a common front against the common threat of international communism. The strategic relationship helped validate the strategy and legitimacy of Latin American militaries by making them part of the US alliance system against communism. The reappraisal is, however, engendering concern among Latin American military establishments as to whether the United States cares about the future security of the region and the missions of the militaries.

The weakening of old alliance structures and the American emphasis on new threats to national security, such as narcotics trafficking and the environmental challenge, have the unintended consequence of intensifying doubts about American intentions. Indeed, these doubts have contributed to a 'new nationalism among the military as a reaction to fear of indiscriminate demilitarization rather than careful restructuring of military institutions'.[6] On 26 March 1992 Assistant Secretary of State for Inter-American Affairs, Bernard Aronson, addressed this concern before the predominantly Latin American faculty and student body of the Inter-American Defense College in Washington, DC. He stated:

- The United States does not seek a new hegemony in the world.
- The United States does not want to weaken or diminish armed forces to its advantage, it is not trying to demilitarise the hemisphere. Nations have a sovereign right to a military; yet reorganisation, as the US is also doing, is a logical step.
- In the war against narcotrafficking there is no signal on the part of the United States of working with the police against the military. Drug trafficking is primarily a police problem. Given the fact that the traffickers are a different and more sophisticated kind of criminal, however, the military needs to help the police.

Aronson's thoughtful comments run counter to the perception among some Latin American officers that the United States wishes to 'control' Latin American militaries in the New World Order. Some officers see more than an element of truth in this because the US political process for security assistance imposes some accountability on the Latin American military. Additionally, there are mixed signals emanating from various US agencies.

The debate about boundaries and the appropriate missions of the Latin American militaries is intense.[7] It joins a global demand for reducing militaries and for turning swords, brigades, warplanes and ships into plowshares, for converting war stocks into peace dividends. In the United States there are calls from senior statesmen, such as Senator Sam Nunn, to have the military prove its social utility by assisting in refurbishing the national infrastructure. His proposed Civil-Military Cooperative Action Program would involve the military in addressing community problems: deficient education, lack of job training, inadequate recreational facilities, and poor health care.[8] While military officials agree with social utility, they will point out that such roles are only legitimate as secondary functions in a dangerous world where combat power is the arbiter and therefore the primary function of warriors.

For a good portion of Latin America, principally Peru, Colombia, and Guatemala (and to a lesser extent, Bolivia, Chile, El Salvador, and Nicaragua) these ideas inform the debate but have less resonance because there is internal conflict. In other countries, social tensions fed by grinding poverty, unwise strategies of drastic economic austerity, and bureaucratic corruption are the conditions that lead to the 'latent insurgency' that the distinguished Peruvian military strategist General Edgardo Mercado Jarrin warned about in the 1960s. They generate hopelessness and delinquency and provide fertile ground for new insurgents, even those animated by high principles of wanting to eliminate corruption and 'irresponsible command'. In Venezuela, on 4 February 1992 and again in November 1992, such conditions contributed to a bloody anti-democratic coup attempt by elements of the Army.[9] In 1989, according to the Economic Commission for Latin America, 40 per cent of Latin America's people lived in poverty, and half of them in extreme poverty. Democracy faces a difficult future if it does not reduce extreme poverty and move towards what the President of the Inter-American Development Bank, Enrique Iglesias, calls 'involving all social groups in the modernization of productive structures.'[10] Thus national security in Latin America frequently involves concern about internal security.

A Brazilian general asserted in October 1992 at the prestigious Escola Superior de Guerra in Rio de Janeiro: 'We have no enemies among our ten neighbours. We are concerned about how to develop our 150 million people. We are concerned with nutrition, health, and education; that's the main objective of our school.' This statement verifies the continuing salience of the security is development doctrine in Latin America. That is: a nation's security is a function of the degree of social, economic, technological, and political development. Such views and supporting strategies have exercised a powerful influence upon military elites in all countries characterised by underdevelopment and ineffective occupation or utilisation of the national territory and its natural and human resources, especially Peru, Ecuador, Argentina, Chile, Venezuela, in addition to Brazil. This developmental nationalism merged quite well with the national security doctrines of the 1960s and 1970s.

Table 1 hypothesises the countries within a spectrum from peace to internal war. Border disputes, such as the one between Peru and Ecuador, hopefully will not lead to international wars in Latin America in the near term. Honduras and El Salvador agreed to the 12 September 1992 judgement of the World Court to settle the dispute over their land border and trilateral control of the Gulf of Fonseca with Nicaragua. This does not deny the legitimate concerns of many countries about the security of land borders, maritime, and space jurisdictions. But most of Latin America's security focus will be internal.

TABLE 1

STRATEGIC CONTEXT: PEACE TO WAR

Peace	Post Conflict Reconstruction & Reconciliation	Some Terrorism and Violence	Internal War
Argentine	El Salvador	Bolivia	Colombia
Brazil	Nicaragua	Chile	Guatemala
Ecuador	Panama	Cuba*	Peru
Mexico		Haiti	
Dominican Republic		Honduras	
Costa Rica		Nicaragua	
Paraguay		Panama	
		Uruguay	
		Venezuela	

Note: *Cuba has institutionalised a system where neither democratic political discourse, nor legitimate dissent are possible. The state practices effective terrorism on its people.

Missions must be relevant to the strategic context and conducted under civilian control. There is a spectrum of civil-military relations in Latin America; from subordination of the military to civilian authority, to a process of transition, to autonomy of military institutions from civilian authority, as follows:

TABLE 2

CIVIL-MILITARY RELATIONS

Subordination	Transition	Autonomy	Elements in Revolt
Colombia	Bolivia	Chile	Venezuela
Cuba[1]	Brazil	El Salvador[2]	
Mexico	Ecuador	Guatemala	
Dominican Republic	Honduras	Haiti	
	Panama (police force)	Nicaragua	
	Paraguay		
	Peru		
	Uruguay		

Notes: 1. Cuba fuses the state, the Communist Party, and the military.
2. Perhaps moving into the transition stage if the peace accord is fully implemented.

The character of these relations will deeply affect how the debate on missions and societal roles will be conducted. In countries undergoing transition from military to civilian government the debate will be even more acute and fraught with danger. It might engender insecurity about the function and permanence of military institutions, as well as suspicions about civilian intentions to subordinate the military to their control and perhaps interfere with the internal workings of the military.

Narcotrafficking

A new menace threatens the social, moral and political fabrics of the Latin American countries – narcotics. Though not classically within the military's purview, narcotics suborn officials, institutions, and governance. Narcotics trafficking makes a mockery of the principle of sovereignty in international order. It also distorts economies and generates violence that often stretches the thin capabilities of poorly trained and poorly paid police forces, which are too often vulnerable to the corrosive attraction of easy money.[11] The military's role is to support the police forces within constitutional limits. The police may not be able to do the job against an enemy that can outgun and outmaneouvre them.

Then too, in Peru, the traffickers are in a *de facto* tactical alliance with the puritanical and barbarous Maoist Shining Path insurgents in the Upper Huallaga Valley – the principal area of coca cultivation in the world.[12] Therefore the counternarcotics effort must be supported by a counterinsurgency designed to win back people and territory from the insurgents and from the cultivation of coca. How to accomplish both without fuelling the insurgency by driving the peasants into the arms of the Shining Path is a serious strategic dilemma.

The struggle against narcotrafficking presents complex challenges to the military professional. First, it calls into question whether soldiers should be involved in the so-called 'drug war'. Counternarcotics clashes with the military's concept of professionalism. As one US Army colonel put it in 1989 (before the US Department of Defense was given the lead role for surveillance and monitoring outside the United States): 'Our job is to vaporize, not to Mirandize.'[13] Such misgivings about police type activities are probably universal among military professionals. Latin American military professionals are no less reluctant. In July 1992, the Sixth Strategic Studies Symposium between delegations from the joint military staffs of Brazil, Uruguay, and Argentina declared its 'obvious disagreement' with 'some sectors in developed countries' (read the United States) about the 'suggestions' made on the 'police roles that Latin American armed forces should basically play.'[14]

Second, the laws and norms of democracies may preclude the military's performing law-enforcement functions of this type. This sensitive and somewhat ambiguous area bears watching because in situations of insurgency and narcotrafficking, such as Peru's, there is a thin line between law enforcement and direct military action. Indeed, Peruvian civilian and military leaders regard the national strategy required to win to be holistic: they need to attack the causes rather than the insurgents and they must summon all the resources of the nation. At the same time, counternarcotics is not a growth industry for the US military looking for new post-Cold War missions. Nor is it much of an opportunity to fatten the defence budget in order to avoid reductions. Similar views prevail among Latin American militaries. There is, however, an acceptance among the Venezuelan, Brazilian, Argentine, Colombian, Peruvian, Bolivian, Ecuadoran, Central American and Mexican militaries that they must support the national effort against the traffickers. The Mexican Army has been involved in the eradication of marijuana fields for many years. Indeed in 1992, according to Mexican military officials, nearly 60 per cent of the Army was involved in the counternarcotics effort. Since 1974, 282 Mexican soldiers and officers have been killed in this unusual war.

Maoism as the New Threat?

Peru's Shining Path (*Sendero Luminoso*) claims to be the remaining legitimate revolutionary alternative in the world. Maoist, ruthless, and well organised, it astutely uses indoctrination, intimidation, and selective violence to eliminate competitors for power and influence. It seeks to establish an autarkic, socialist utopia bereft of the bourgeois trappings of democracy. Its political-military doctrine stresses a long war designed to wear down the government, the military, and intermediate institutions. As the Shining Path remains on the ascendancy, and threatens to defeat the government, the movement may well become a new model of revolutionary action for the dissident left in Latin America. Yet its brutal tactics combined with the strong cult of personality surrounding its now captive leader, Abimael Guzman, indicate weakness rather than strength.

Despite these limitations, the Peruvian government has not found an effective strategy to counter it, proving that power is indeed situational and dynamic. Though in 1992 there were increasing reports of Shining Path international activities, exporting its revolutionary strategy appeared to be a low priority. Nevertheless, the social conditions that help sustain the legitimacy of revolutionary violence in Peru (a legitimacy proclaimed even by President Alberto Fujimori), where nearly half (12 million) of the population has no money to buy food, also exist elsewhere in Latin America. One is reminded of Boston University scholar David Scott Palmer's comment that insurgents do not succeed, but governments fail.[15] The capture of Guzman in September 1992 removed the aura of invincibility from the Shining Path, but its defeat may be a distant prospect.

What Should be the Spectrum of Missions?

There has always been tension between the missions of external and internal security. Two examples are pertinent. Colombian President Cesar Gaviria Trujillo told the 1991 graduating class of the military academy: 'The military forces have as their principal goal the defense of sovereignty, the independence, the territorial integrity of the nation, and constitutional order.'[16] In El Salvador the agreement on the armed forces purge and reforms, signed in Mexico City on 16 January 1992, reaffirmed the constitutional provision that the armed forces are a 'permanent' institution that serves the nation. The agreement (full text in appendix) goes on to differentiate between national defence and security. It is the same distinction made in the Brazilian constitution of 1988 and the National Defense Act of 1988 in Argentina. In the words of the Salvadoran document:

> The armed forces doctrine is based on the distinction between the concepts of security and defense. National defense, a responsibility of the armed forces, is aimed at guaranteeing sovereignty and territorial integrity in the face of a foreign threat. Security, though part of the aforementioned notion, is a broader concept based on full respect for societal and individual rights. In addition to national defense, security encompasses economic, political, and social aspects that go beyond the constitutional authority of the armed forces, and whose responsibility is that of other sectors of society and the state.
>
> The preservation of internal peace, tranquility, order, and public security is outside the ordinary mission of the armed forces as an institution responsible for national defense. In such instances, any eventual use of the armed forces is absolutely unusual, to be exercised only when ordinary means have been exhausted, . . .

While the Salvadoran statement presents the ideal distinction of the military's circumscribed role in national defence, the reality and practice elsewhere often is quite different. Nation building, especially the task of providing a presence where civilian agencies are either incapable or reluctant to go to, is an important function. The Brazilian Army's Amazon Military Command, as an example, performs a spectrum of missions in the remote hinterlands of the Amazon. It builds roads and airports, establishes settlements, cooperates in economic development, builds schools, provides education, health services, mail service and transportation, in addition to internal and external security.[17] Such activities were part of the mission of the US Army in the conquest of the West in the nineteenth century. The US Army's Corps of Engineers retains the mission of taking care of waterways and constitutes a model of the nation-building military in the Third World. Often little can be accomplished in the remote interior of a country without the administrative and logistical support of the military. This is the case in Peru, Ecuador, Colombia, Paraguay, Chile, Bolivia, Venezuela, and the Antarctic territories claimed by Argentina and Chile. There ought to be limits to nation-building activities, however, so that civilians assume these functions as soon as possible and without having to compete with the military. Nor should military institutions be managing industrial enterprises that have little to do with their professional and constitutional responsibilities.

The Missions

It is remarkable that the fundamental missions of military institutions are little changed for the post-Cold War era. Although they may vary in their emphasis from one country to another, they generally are to:

- Defend sovereign borders, maritime zones, and air space.
- Control emergent insurgencies.
- Help develop national infrastructures without competing with civilians in activities in which civilians can do the job.
- Help civilian authorities preserve natural resources and fight environmental pollution.
- Assist in handling natural disasters, international peacekeeping, and modest participation in multinational operations such as 'Desert Shield' and 'Desert Storm'. (Argentina sent ships and troops to the Persian Gulf during 'Desert Shield' and 'Desert Storm', while Honduras offered to do so. Six Chilean helicopters and crews and about 22 military observers from Argentina, Uruguay, and Venezuela serve with the United Nation Iraq/Kuwait observer mission. Argentine battalions participate in peacekeeping in Croatia and Cyprus. Peacekeeping is an important aspect of these nations' foreign policies and helps to legitimate the other missions of the military in the eyes of civilian society.)

- Provide a symbol of nationality and sovereignty, as is done almost universally by military institutions. (This ought not to be a monopoly of the military, however, for civilians have been at least equally instrumental in the national history.)
- Advise civilian authorities as well as regional organisations such as the Organization of American States and the United Nations in technical aspects of international conflict resolution and verification of arms control arrangements.
- Assist law enforcement authorities in counternarcotics efforts.

Of all these missions, the fundamental ones must be the first two. Without the external defence responsibility and the mission to be prepared to deal with insurgencies, the militaries would be essentially reduced to boy scout troops and municipal bands. Defence of the nation from external enemies is the irreducible *sine qua non* legitimating function of the armed forces. These sentiments are understandably troubling to concerned citizens in societies trying to democratise or redemocratise after years of military rule, such as El Salvador, Uruguay, Argentina, Chile, and Brazil. The Panamanian people, after being subjected to military thuggery for 21 years under Generals Omar Torrijos and Manuel Antonio Noriega, voted in November 1992 on a constitutional referendum that included the abolition of the military. (The referendum was defeated, but the 'no' vote was interpreted as a 'no' against the weak performance of the Guillermo Endara government, rather than a vote to recreate the military.) Costa Rica under Pepe Figueres made that commitment in the late 1940s. Panama's and Costa Rica's circumstances are unusual and hardly apply to other countries.

To deny the external defence and security missions is the equivalent of disbanding the military institution. Managing such denial on the part of civilians would be so difficult as to be a prescription for another round of coups. It can also be argued that taking on international peacekeeping roles requires a high level of military operational readiness, as the experience of the Canadian Armed Forces indicates during numerous such missions around the globe. Peacekeeping missions help validate the legitimate defense responsibilities of the institutions before their societies back home. This rationale helps drive the Argentine Army's extensive peacekeeping commitment in Bosnia.

The Military Budgets

Latin American defence expenditures are among the lowest in the world, as the tables on pages 159–161 indicate. Economic austerity in

Latin America has seriously affected military budgets. Budgets ought to be a function of the military strategy requirements of a state. In some instances the reductions in budget are so drastic as to exacerbate tension between civilians and the military. A case in point is Brazil. Between 1985 and 1990, Brazilian defence expenditures were reduced by 75 per cent, resulting in serious problems of readiness and morale. Reflecting these concerns, Navy Minister Mario Cesar Flores remarked in April 1992: 'The time has come for Brazilian society to decide on the destiny that it wants to give to its armed forces.'[18]

Democratic civil-military relations require that defence budgets evolve from joint consultations between civilians and military. It is assumed in these consultations that expenditures will reflect military strategy. Frequently, however, the military budget and strategy are also expressions of the armed forces' interest in survival and growth. Stated in other terms, the military strategy will reflect not simply legitimate defence needs but also the military's self-interest in survival with dignity and societal respect. This is not an uncommon position among bureaucracies and institutions. The policy challenge is to strike the appropriate balance between the resources required for a credible military strategy and the minimum required for institutional survival.

The New Security Dialogue

Interstate conflict should be a thing of the past now that the legitimacy of democratic principles is on the ascendancy and economic integration in the form of North American Free Trade Area, Enterprise for the Americas Initiative, and Mercosur[19] has gained momentum. In alluding to this, Domingo Cavallo, the Argentine Foreign Minister, in August 1990 told his country's future military leaders to 'Take into account . . . the common interests of future security and of eliminating costly defensive systems for risks that no longer exist.' The recent efforts (December 1991–January 1992) by Ecuador and Peru to find a solution to their border dispute supplements those of Argentina and Chile to delineate the last remaining portions of their Andean boundary. Peru and Bolivia also agreed to an outlet for the latter at the Peruvian port of Ilo, while Peru and Chile are implementing the final provisions of the 1929 Treaty of Ancon.

Significant also is the December 1991 Vienna agreement between Brazil and Argentina on safeguards against nuclear proliferation. The agreement culminates a process of wresting away control over the two countries' nuclear development programmes from their respective military establishments.[20] Additionally, the Organization of American

States has elevated the discussion of the national security requirements of Latin American democracies to a higher level of concern. These are welcome developments for regional peace and security because they move the interstate dialogue away from fruitless confrontation to cooperation and regional economic integration. Moreover, it is generally true that democratic governments, fully confident of their accountability to the governed, are more amenable to peaceful solutions of international conflict than are narrowly based governments. Such linkage augurs well for democracy and security in the future.

The redefinition and modernisation of missions and roles must take into account the need to reduce the distance between civilians and military in the interest of promoting greater democratic harmony. For reasons that are deeply imbedded in history, a no-man's land divides the two, leading to suspicion, fear, and paranoia – not a healthy state of affairs for democracy. *Se puede militarizar a un civil pero no se puede civilizar a un militar.* 'You can militarize a civilian but you cannot civilize a soldier' is a prevailing description of civilian attitudes.

If he were alive today Clemenceau would probably recognise that modern defence requirements are so challenging and complex that cooperation between civilians and the military is even more fundamental than it was back in his day. Such cooperation is critical in winning the struggle against narcotraffickers, terrorists, and insurgents. The military cannot win these 'low-intensity conflicts' alone. Winning requires summoning the full resources of the nation to the common effort. The distinguished Peruvian novelist and unsuccessful 1990 presidential candidate Mario Vargas Llosa addressed this strategic imperative:

> The counterterrorist struggle for democracy will only be won if military men and civilians participate in it, shoulder to shoulder, knowing that the result of this conflict will decide whether Peru will have a future as a civilised or as a barbarous state. My great conviction is that we, the large majority of Peruvians who believe in liberty, are until now losing it because the civilian authorities have not assumed the responsibility that corresponds to them, have not known how to mobilise public opinion to decisively support the counter-subversive action, they have not given to the forces of order the political guidance and the indispensable logistical means for them to act and the civilians have not recognised the extreme challenge which terrorism represents for the future and the present moment of our country.[21]

The most compelling challenge for democracy in Latin America is not only to integrate the military more fully into society, but to bring these institutions under prudent civilian control. The task will not be accomplished either by wishful thinking or by attempts to strip down the military. Such an approach may feed the paranoia that will nurture coups. The task will require mutual education and responsible dialogue on national and defence affairs. Nothing less than a cultural revolution in university education and professional military formation is required to modernise both civilian and military attitudes and capabilities.

Equally important is bringing the military out of the intellectual and cultural closet. Much could be accomplished by elevating the military academies, from which the officer corps originate, to university levels of education. Argentina's military reform implements such a visionary concept of professional military education. It envisages two tracks for officer development, both requiring university degrees – either in international relations or in engineering. University level education is the norm for armed forces in the United States, Canada, Western Europe, Asia, and elsewhere. The professionalisation of the new police force in Panama and of the postwar military and police in El Salvador also contemplates university level training for officers.[22]

If these measures are taken, the foundation will be established for more harmonious relations between civilians and military and, thereby, possibly stronger democracies. If, as the result of defence cuts, the military is again marginalised and relegated to the sterile environments of the barracks and training grounds, regional security and democracy will again be at risk. Isolation from society and from the international community is a serious threat to both military professionalism and harmonious civil-military relations.

Implications for US Policy: Advice for Constructive Engagement

US policy needs to be sensitive to this danger and not advocate a quick and unsophisticated fix in the size, roles, and missions of the Latin American armies, navies, and air forces. Those attributes should be the outcome of the democratic civil-military dialogue within Latin America and should not be imposed from outside. The United States should not spare Latin America the experience, the exhilaration and, yes, the frustration that ensues from learning on its own. Moreover, it is not clear that we can be that decisive in a civil-military dialogue that must be uniquely Latin American. Forty years of security assistance programmes confirm that access to Latin American military institutions is neither power nor political influence, either in peacetime or war, whether in the Army of Venezuela in February 1992, in Noriega's corrupt Panamanian Defense Forces, or in the Salvadoran officer corps during the internal war of the 1980s. Yet, US security assistance did eventually have a strategic payoff in the democratic principles now being implemented in El Salvador. Equally clear is that no access is the path to misperception and potential disaster. We should be attentive to the debate and the process of redefining roles and missions and be willing to assist when called upon to either advise or help train Latin America's future national security professionals.

For such assistance to be credible and acceptable, US policy must recognise both the fundamental external and internal defense responsibilities of the Latin American militaries and the leadership role of civilian authority. If posited otherwise, such assistance may be neither credible nor welcome. This is a tall order for Americans, for we have been reluctant to recognise the defence role of the Latin American militaries. We have done so when we needed them for strategic purposes. At the same time, it can be argued that the United States is the only player that, through the instrument of military assistance, can impose some accountability on the various militaries, particularly those that are dependent on us for equipment, training, and political support. How the militaries and their civilian counterparts deal with this will help shape the possibilities for reducing the 'low-intensity conflict' between Washington and Latin America on the appropriate strategy for winning the wars against drugs and insurgents and for promoting democratic military professionalism.

There is the danger that since the traditional strategic imperative for US cooperation with the Latin American militaries has vanished, it will become more difficult to sustain a sophisticated strategy of constructive engagement built on professional communication, training, and military to military relations. The United States is itself reducing its military and reconsidering its commitments around the globe. The small and low visibility military to military initiatives that underpinned the professional dialogue and served as a conduit for political communication between the United States and Latin American militaries may fall by the wayside. There appears to be, for example, a reluctance in the US Congress and elsewhere in the policy community to support assistance to the Salvadoran armed forces that would facilitate an intelligent 50 per cent drawdown and follow-on democratic reforms and professionalisation, as mandated by the 16 January 1992 Peace Accord. This is a form of strategic disengagement that has come back to haunt us in the recent past.

There is also the strategic dissonance generated by the 'drug war', which threatens to overwhelm the dialogues on the legitimate defence responsibilities of the militaries and the appropriate strategy for winning what Peruvian analyst Gustavo Gorriti calls the 'democratic counter-insurgency'.[23] These contradictions are salient in the stalemate in US policy for Peru, which, until the 5 April 1992 *autogolpe*, was willing to provide law enforcement aid for counternarcotics and help strengthen Peru's institutional capabilities, but provide no military aid for the counterinsurgency. Such an approach was prudent given the American experience with supporting friends in the field, such as Vietnam and El Salvador. It was very consistent with the American concept of the 'just war' in ambiguous warfare.

An Agenda For Caution and Pragmatism

Relieved of the straitjacket of the Cold War the United States and Latin American countries have an opportunity to reshape their relations. The future should be an era of strategic creativity and cooperation in the common pursuit of peace, economic development, and democracy. There is a risk that as the complex US political process turns inwards during the Bill Clinton administration, mixed signals will once again emerge from Washington. The ongoing debate on the size of the defence budget and military roles and missions should not transmit the notion that the United States wishes to either 'demilitarise', control, or turn the armed forces of Latin America into anti-narcotics police. Yet, the US policy apparatus is fully capable of mixing signals. As an example, the United States Southern Command, the Panama-based unified command, needs to correct the imbalance in its current emphasis on the drug war. That emphasis, congenial to the command and to institutional support in Washington, does not address the core interests of the Latin American military professional. Additionally, there is no natural constituency in Washington for the policy of 'constructive engagement'. Accordingly, the United States needs to engage more fully the diversity of foreign policy and military agencies in promoting democratic military professionalism. Initiatives such as the International Fellows programmes at the various US War Colleges, civilian participation in the International Military Education and Training Program, and intensive exchanges between subject matter experts can pay handsome dividends.

NOTES

The views expressed are those of the author and do not necessarily reflect the official policy or position of the Department of the Army, the Department of Defense, or the US

Government. An earlier version of this article was prepared for the United Nations Regional Seminar on Non-Proliferation and Confidence and Security Building Measures, Asunción, Paraguay, 18–20 Jan. 1993.

 1. Adm. J.C. Wylie, 'Assumptions Underlying a General Theory', from Wylie, *Military Strategy: A General Theory of Power Control* (Rutgers, NJ: Rutgers UP, 1967), p.78.
 2. The core national interests are explicated in Donald Neuchterlein, *America Recommitted: United States National Interests in a Restructured World* (Lexington: UP of Kentucky, 1991). His concept of national interests has been adapted by the US Army War College (hereafter USAWC) in its strategy planning exercises. The literature on national power and military strategy is vast. This author owes much intellectual debt to Hans Morgenthau, Samuel Huntington, Henry Kissinger, Carl von Clausewitz, James Dougherty, and to contemporary proponents of international order and the just theory of war.
 3. See Joseph Nye, *Bound to Lead: The Changing Nature of American Power* (NY: Basic Books, 1990).
 4. Caspar W. Weinberger, 'The Uses of Military Power', *Defense '85*, Arlington, VA: Armed Forces Info. Service, Jan. 1985.
 5. For a more complete statement of the evolving strategy see Colin L. Powell, *National Military Strategy of the United States* (Washington, DC: US EPO, 1992).
 6. Constantino Urcuyo, 'Civil-Military Relations at the End of the Cold War', Rapporteur's Report on the Conference, Asunción, Paraguay, 23–24 April 1992, p.2.
 7. E.g., the Sept.–Oct. 1992 issue of the Spanish language edition of *Military Review* is entirely devoted to the question of the roles and missions of the military, particularly the Latin American, in the 'new world order'. See also: Virgilio Rafael Beltran, 'Looking for New Roles for Latin American Armies', paper presented at the Interim Conference of the Int'l Congress of Military Sociology, Armed Forces and Conflict Resolution, Valparaiso, Chile, 29–31 Aug. 1992. A version of the same paper is the lead article in the aforementioned *Military Review*. See also the new and promising journal *Sequridad Estrategica Regional*, published in Buenos Aires by Senator Eduardo Pedro Vaca, member of the Argentine Senate, and Luis Tibiletti, with the support of numerous research centres and university groups in the region.
 8. See also Col. Philip A. Brehm and Maj. Wilbur E. Gray, 'Alternative Missions for the US Army', USAWC, Stategic Studies Inst. (hereafter SSI) 17 June 1992; Brian J. Ohlinger, 'Peacetime Engagement: A Search for Relevance?' USAWC, SSI, 15 Oct. 1992.
 9. Michael Coppedge, 'Venezuela's Vulnerable Democracy', *Journal of Democracy*, 3/4 (Oct. 1992), pp.32–44.
10. Enrique Iglesias, 'The Human Face of Economic Adjustment', *The IDB* (June 1992), p.6.
11. For advice from a Colombian Army officer on how the military should deal with the potential problem of corruption from drugs see: Lt. Col. Carlos A. Velasquez, 'Protecting the Ethics of Subordinates in the War Against Narcotrafficking: A New Challenge for Commanders', *Military Review* Spanish language ed. (Sept.–Oct. 1992), pp.81–5.
12. The nature of this relationship is debated. It is fair to say that the Shining Path exacts payments from the narcotraffickers to use airfields in the Upper Huallaga Valley. The insurgents also protect the coca farmers from exploitation by the traffickers. The Shining Path strenuously denies participating in the drug trade. See: Cynthia McClintock, 'Opportunities and Constraints to Source Reduction of Coca: The Peruvian Socio-Political Context', George Washington Univ., Dept. of Political Science, April 1992.
13. Mirandize refers to a procedural requirement imposed by American courts (Miranda vs. Arizona, 1966) on the police to warn an individual of his constitutional rights as soon as he is effectively in custody, such as the rights to remain silent and to have an attorney. Therefore, the unnamed US Army colonel stated that his profession is not

that of policeman. For a more rigorous analysis of the legal dimensions of the military's role in the 'drug war' and its implications for US civil-military relations, see: Maj. Peter M. Sanchez, ' "Drug War": The US Military and National Security', *Air Force Law Review*, Vol.34.

14. Argentine Joint Chief of Staff Adm. Emilio Jose Osses, 'Military Cooperation Within Mercosur Context', *La Nacion*, 8 July 1992, p.9, as reported in *Foreign Broadcast Information Service, Latin America* [hereafter FBIS, LA] 17 July, 1992, p.1.
15. For more information on Shining Path, see the outstanding collection of papers in David Scott Palmer, ed. [See review in *SW&I* 3/3, Winter 1992, pp.319–21]. *The Shining Path of Peru* (NY: St Martin's Press, 1992). For the Peruvian military's analysis of the insurgency see, Ejercito Peruano, Escuela Superior de Guerra, *Defensa Interna: Movimientos Subversivos en el Peru* (Chorrillos, 1991). For a description of the complex nexus between coca farmers, traffickers, the Shining Path, and the government's strategy see, Adm. Jorge Hesse, 'The Peruvian Naval Forces in the Struggle Against Subversion and Drug Trafficking in the Amazonian Region of Ucayali', *TVI Report* (Summer 1992), pp.30–8; and Thomas Kamm, 'Valley in Peru Provides a Glimpse of Things to Come: Government Intensifies War On Rebels, but Residents Get Caught in Middle'. *Wall Street Journal*, 8 April 1992, p.A17. A pessimistic view of the government's capability to defeat Shining Path is Gordon H. McCormick, *From the Sierra to the Cities: the Urban Campaign of the Shining Path* (Santa Monica: RAND Corporation, 1992. [Also reviewed in *SW&I* 3/3].
16. Palabras del Señor Presidente de la Republica Doctor Cesar Gaviria Trujillo, en el Acto de Graduacion de la Escuela Militar de Cadetes 'General Jose Maria Cordova', 5 Dec. 1991, *Revista de las Fuerzas Armadas* (Colombia), No.141 (Oct.–Nov. 1991), p.11.
17. For an authoritative analysis of the role of the Brazilian Army in the Amazon, see Lt. Col. Paulo Caesar Miranda de Azevedo, 'Security of the Brazilian Amazon Area', Carlisle, PA: USAWC, Military Studies Paper, April 1992; for the Ecuadorean Army's role in development, see Lt. Col. Luis Hernandez, 'The Ecuadorean Army, Security and Development in the 90s', Carlisle, PA: USAWC, Military Studies Paper, 26 March 1992. See also the various papers published by the Brazilian Army's Command and Staff College's Ceatso Brasileiro de Estudos Estrategicos in *A Amazonia Brasileira: Simposio FEBRES-ECEME* (Oct. 1991). Some deal with military presence and defence of the Amazon and reflect the military's deep sensitivity about international publicity about ecological damage.
18. Cited in 'The Uproar Over Soldiers' Pay', *ISTOE SENHOR*, 22 April 1992, in FBIS, LA, 3 June 1992, p.32.
19. Mercosur is the Free Trade Zone encompassing Argentina, Brazil, Uruguay, and Paraguay.
20. See Eugene Robinson, 'Brazil and Argentina Step Back From the Nuclear Brink', *Washington Post* National Weekly ed., 3–9 Feb. 1992.
21. 'Civiles y Militares en el Peru de la Libertad', speech given to the Centro de Altos Estudios Militares, Barranco, Lima, 25 Feb. 1990, p.5.
22. On Argentina's military education reform see Jorge Grecco and Gustavo Gonzalez, *Argentina: el Ejercito que tenemos* (Buenos Aires; Editorial Sudamericana, 1990); Escuela Superior de Guerra, Ejercito Argentino, *Education in the Argentine Army–Officer's Career Plan*, (Buenos Aires, 1991).
23. Gustavo Gorriti, 'Latin America's Internal Wars', *Journal of Democracy* 2/1 (Winter 1991), pp.85–98.

APPENDIX
AGREEMENT ON ARMED FORCES PURGE, REFORMS

SAN SALVADOR, 13 JANUARY 1992

Following is the full text of the agreement on reforms and purge of the Salvadoran armed forces, one of the most important peace accords achieved by the government and the guerrillas, which will be signed on 16 January in Mexico.

Like the other documents, this document on the armed forces, which has not been previously disclosed, contains points that are pending negotiation in the talks that were extended again 13 January in New York.

I. DOCTRINAL PRINCIPLES OF THE ARMED FORCES

The armed forces doctrine, based on the constitutional reforms approved in April 1991, will conform to the following principles, which from now on will be based exclusively on the armed forces' institutional administration and education system; and its actions will be restricted to the strict observance of the same:

A. The armed forces have the mission of defending state sovereignty and territorial integrity, under the terms of administration defined by the constitution and the law. Compliance with same goes together with democratic values and strict adherence to the constitution in every aspect.

B. As established by the constitution, the armed forces is a permanent institution that serves the nation; it is obedient, professional, non-political, and nondeliberating. Its institutional administration and actions will also conform to principles resulting from the state of law; the supremacy of human dignity and respect for individual rights; respect and defense of the sovereignty of the Salvadoran people; the notion of the armed forces as an institution alien to every political, ideological, or social bias and any other form of discrimination; and the subordination of the institution to constitutional authorities.

C. The armed forces must respect the political order established by the sovereign will of the people and every political or social change resulting from it, in keeping with the democratic procedures listed in the constitution. Its institutional administration and actions will be defined to insure friendly relations with civilian society, as well as the normal development of its members.

D. As a government institution, the armed forces has an instrumental, not decision-making, character in the political arena. Consequently, only the President of the Republic and the basic government organs will be able to use the armed forces to fulfill the provisions adopted. Within their respective constitutional areas of authority. This will ensure full compliance with the constitution. In addition, the aforementioned authorities will be exclusively responsible for verifying that the political and social changes mentioned in the paragraph above will be included in the constitution.

E. The armed forces doctrine is based on the distinction between the concepts of security and defense. National defense, a responsibility of the armed forces, is aimed at guaranteeing sovereignty and territorial integrity in the face of a foreign military threat. Security, though part of the aforementioned notion, is a broader concept based on full respect for societal and individual rights. In addition to national defense, security encompasses economic, political, and social aspects that go beyond the constitutional authority of the armed forces, and whose responsibility is that of other sectors of society and the state.

F. The preservation of internal peace, tranquility, order, and public security is outside the ordinary mission of the armed forces as an institution responsible for national defense. In such instances, any eventual use of the armed forces is absolutely unusual, to be exercised only when ordinary means have been exhausted, and under the terms established by the constitutional reforms approved in April 1991.

II. EDUCATIONAL SYSTEM OF THE ARMED FORCES

Reiterating the full extent of its previous agreements, whereby the professional training of the members of the armed forces will emphasize the importance of human dignity and democratic values, respect for human rights, and the institution's subordination to the constitutional authorities; the parties have reached the following agreements:

A. The legal framework of the educational and training system of the armed forces will be drafted based on what has been established by articles 212 and 213 of the constitutional reform agreed to in April 1991.

B. The doctrinal framework of the educational system of the armed forces is defined by the doctrinale principles described in Chapter I of this agreement. Such principles will be the basis of all educational and training programs of the armed forces at all levels.

C. The plans and programs of study aimed at the education and training of the armed forces will include, in addition to technical-military subjects, scientific and humanistic courses aimed at integral training; which will provide the students with the necessary background to participate in the country's institutional life and encourage a permanent harmonious relation with civilian society, as well as the student's normal development as one of its members.

D. To contribute to the efforts of achieving the objectives mentioned in the preceding paragraph, the members of the armed forces will be encouraged to take professional and graduate courses taught by the country's universities.

E. The military academy will have a collegiate regimen in educational matters and its director will be the president of an academic council, formed by military and civilian professors. The members of the academic council will be appointed by the president of the republic.

F. The national commission for the consolidation of peace (COPAZ) will decide on the number of members of the academic council, which will be jointly composed of civilian and military members.

G. The civilian components of the academic council will be appointed by the president, based on criteria of political pluralism, from groups of three candidates proposed by COPAZ.

H. The teaching body will be appointed by the academic council, which will ensure that no single political tendency prevails.

I. The Director of the Military Academy will be appointed by the President of the Republic.

J. The admission system will be determined by the academic council and will ensure it is not discriminatory.

K. COPAZ will supervise the compliance of Sections G, H, and J, under the terms stipulated in the 25 September 1991 New York agreement.

III. PURGING

A purging process within the armed forces has been agreed upon in the framework of the peace agreements to accomplish the supreme objective of a national reconciliation based on the evaluation of all its members by an ad hoc commission.

A. The evaluation will consider the background of each officer, including: 1. His record of observance of the law, with a special emphasis on respect for human rights, both in his personal conduct as well as with the strictness he may have ordered the correction and punishment of human rights violations or abuses which may have occured under his supervision; 2. His professional capabilities; 3. His ability to conduct himself under the new conditions of peace within the context of a democratic society, as well as to promote the democratization of the country, guarantee a strict respect for human rights, and reunify Salvadoran society, which is the common goal of the parties in the Geneva agreement. The existence of serious deficiencies in any one of the aspects mentioned above, is sufficient grounds for the decisions that must be made by the ad hoc commission according to paragraph G of this chapter.

B. The evaluation will be done by a strictly impartial *ad hoc* commission, formed by three Salvadorans known for their independence and unblemished democratic background. Two armed forces officers of unblemished professional performance will also participate. They will only participate in the commission's deliberations, not in the investigatory phase. They will, however, have access to the findings of the commission.

The selection of the three civilian members of the ad hoc commission will be a result of consultations carried out by the UN Secretary-General, who is to inform the two sides on the same date about the results of this process. The President of the Republic will issue, within five days following this agreement, the document legalizing the commission. The same procedure is to be followed to fill a vacancy in the commission. The President will appoint the two armed forces officers who will participate in the *ad hoc* commission.

C. The Truth Commission (*Comision De La Verdad*), created by the Mexican Accords of 26 April 1991 (henceforth 'The Truth Commission') may appoint an observer to the *ad hoc* commission.

D. The *ad hoc* commission will have the civilian support personnel it deems necessary.

E. The defense and public security ministry, as well as any other public entity, will provide any information requested by the ad hoc commission, including the service record of every officer. In every case, the *ad hoc* commission may use information from any other source it deems reliable.

F. The *ad hoc* commission will adopt and, if need be, request all the measures it deems necessary to protect itself, as well as to protect the physical and moral well-being of individuals, regardless of their position.

G. The *ad hoc* commission will adopt its conclusions, following a meeting with the persons involved, based on the terms established in paragraph A of this chapter. The conclusions may range from a change of command (*destino*) to, if appropriate, the discharge of the serviceman under review.

H. The *ad hoc* commission will strive to adopt unanimous decisions. If that is not possible, a majority vote will be sufficient.

I. The evaluation will be extended to NCO personnel if the *ad hoc* commission recommends it.

J. The *ad hoc* commission will conclude its review within three months. Administrative decisions based on the findings of the evaluation will be adopted within 30 days following the date the government is notified and will implemented within 60 days from the same date.

K. The results of the evaluation will not hamper the enforcement of recommendations by the Truth Commission.

IV. REDUCTION

The new reality of peace will result in a reduction in the armed forces. Its scope will be adjusted to the functions assigned by the constitution, within the framework of the constitutional amendments from the Mexican Accords, as well as to its doctrine. In view of the above, and in implementing the New York agreements, the government has submitted to the UN Secretary-General a plan for the reduction of the armed forces. The Secretary-General has informed the Farabundo Marti National Liberation Front about the plan. The implementation of this plan should produce, as a practical consequence, the reduction of the different branches of the armed forces.

A. ORGANIZATION: The organization of the armed forces will correspond to its institutional mission in peacetime, with an arrangement of the functions assigned to it by the constitution, that entails:

1. The appropriate unit to fulfill different tasks corresponding to said mission;
2. The appropriate structure, organization, and equipment in terms of weapons, service, category (rank), and specialty; and
3. The personnel needs, according to unit, mission, and rank.

B. UNITS:

1. The reduction of the units will be based on the new organization of the armed forces. The number and kind of units will be adjusted to said organization.
2. In every case, the reduction covers units created as a result of the conflict.

C. PERSONNEL: The new organization and the reduction of the units entail the reduction of armed forces personnel in various categories, branches, services, or specialties. The number of officers will be reduced in line with the reduction plan and in accordance with the normal needs of an army.

D. MATERIAL AND EQUIPMENT: Material and equipment will be adapted to the new organization, to the new doctrine of the armed forces, and their constitutional mission.

E. INSTALLATIONS: The reduction entails the recoversion, return, or elimination of installations that will no longer be used by the armed forces.

F. ADMINISTRATIVE AND SERVICE STRUCTURES: All the administrative and service structures will be adapted to the new reality of peace and to the doctrine and new constitutional mission of the armed forces.

G. MILITARY EXPENDITURES (Pending)

V. OVERCOMING OF IMPUNITY

It is recognized that all assertions of impunity of armed forces officers must be clarified and overcome, especially in cases in which respect for human rights is involved. To this end, the sides remit to the Truth Commission the analysis and solution of this point. All without detriment to the principle, which the sides equally recognize, that incidents of this nature, regardless of the sector from which their perpetrators come, must be the object of exemplary action by the courts of justice, so that the penalties established by the law will be applied against those who are found to be responsible.

VI. PUBLIC SECURITY CORPS

A. In accordance with the constitutional reform stemming from the Mexico agreements, the National Civilian Police (PNC), which will be under the direction of civilian authorities, will be in charge of preserving public security, order, calm, and peace in both urban and rural areas. The PNC and the armed forces will be independent and will be under different ministries.

B. Under the terms of the agreement the sides will sign on this same date, the PNC will be a new body, with a new organization, new cadres, new education and training mechanisms, and a new doctrine.

C. The National Guard and the treasury police will be eliminated as public security corps. Their members will be incorporated into the army.

VII. INTELLIGENCE SERVICES

A. The National Intelligence Directorate will be eliminated and state intelligence services will be entrusted to a new institution that will be called the State Intelligence Organization (*Organismo De Inteligencia Del Estado*). It will be subordinated to civilian power, under the direct authority of the President of the Republic. During the transition period, the Director of the State Intelligence Organization will be a civilian appointed by the President of the Republic on the basis of broad acceptance. The Director can be removed by the legislative assembly for grave violations of human rights.

B. The legal regime, the training of personnel, organization guidelines, operational directives, and, in general, the doctrine of the state intelligence organization will fall within the framework of democratic principles; of the concept that state intelligence is a function of the state for the common good, free of any consideration for politics, ideology, or social position or any other discrimination; and of strict respect for human rights.

C. The activities of the state intelligence organization must be confined to what is required for the gathering and analysis of information in the general interest, by the means and within the limits authorized by the legal order and, particularly, with strict respect for human rights.

D. The activities of the state intelligence organization will be supervised by the legislative assembly, in accordance with the control mechanisms established by the constitution.

E. Employment and compensation options will be offered to those personnel currently working for the national intelligence directorate who are not incorporated into the new state intelligence organization. International support will be requested for this purpose.

F. The incorporation into the state intelligence organization of the national intelligence directorate personnel who so request it will be possible only after rigorous evaluation of their background, capabilities, and aptitude to adapt to the new doctrine. This evaluation will be conducted by the director of the organization, under the authority of the president of the republic, with the support of international advice and verification by the United Nations.

G. The state intelligence organization will be organized by its director, under the authority of the president of the republic.

VIII. RAPID DEPLOYMENT INFANTRY BATTALIONS

It is accepted that the rapid deployment infantry battalions were formed at a specific point in the conflict and that their existence should be reviewed in the measure that circumstances allow. It is, consequently, also accepted that the rapid deployment infantry battalions will not be necessary in the new reality of peace and, thus, can be liquidated and their personnel relocated.

IX. SUBORDINATION TO CIVILIAN POWER

The President of the Republic, within the discretionary authority bestowed on him by the constitution, will be able to appoint civilians to the position of Defense Minister. In this respect, the persons appointed should agree to comply with the peace agreements.

X. PARAMILITARY ORGANIZATIONS

A. It is accepted that all organizations or paramilitary groups must be banned in a state of law.

B. Civil defense: The civil defense force will be liquidated, gradually and subject to the implementation schedule of the peace agreements.

C. Armed Forces Reserves: A new armed forces reserve system will replace the current territorial service and will operate according to the following terms:

1. The armed forces reserves will have the responsibility of organizing and operating the following: (1) An up-to-date register on the citizens who are in the reserves and of those who are suited for military service; (2) A system to update the reserve personnel's military skills; (3) Procedures to call up reserve personnel when they are required to enter active duty to carry out the mission assigned to the armed forces by the constitution.
2. The new armed forces reserves will be under the defense ministry.
3. The armed forces reserves will only carry out missions once they have entered active duty and in conformity with the constitution. It will not carry out public security or population and territory control tasks.
4. The valid laws, regulations, and decrees on this subject must be made to agree with the terms stipulated in the current agreement.

D. Regulations for private security services: The parties admit the need to regulate the activities of all those organizations, groups, or people who give security or protection services to individuals, firms, or state institutions, so as to ensure the openness of the private security services' activities, as well as their strict adherence to the law and respect for human rights. To this effect:

1. A special law will regulate the activities of the organizations, groups, or people who give security or protection to indivi-

duals, firms, or state institutions. Said law will establish the requirements to offer and to render such services: A public record of their personnel, weapons, and different offices, if they should have them; of the groups, organizations, or people rendering private security services; the establishment of appropriate control mechanisms, which may be supervised by the national civilian police; and, in general, the necessary restrictions and constraints to ensure that private security services operate entirely within the law.

2. The law will also establish peremptory deadlines to comply with the aforementioned requirements whenever pertinent. The organizations that have not complied with the aforementioned requirements once the deadline has passed will be considered lawless and its members and organizers will be subject to the corresponding legal penalties.

3. To this effect, the parts agreed on in the outline for the legislative bill are included as an annex to the current agreement and are being sent to COPAZ, with other considerations, so that COPAZ may prepare the corresponding bill.

XI. SUSPENSION OF FORCIBLE RECRUITMENT

A. Any form of forcible recruitment will be suspended when the end of the armed confrontation becomes effective, until such time the law referred to in the subsequent paragraph is enacted.

B. A new law on military service and reserves will be promulgated. This law will establish the following basic tenets of military service: The universal, obligatory, nondiscriminatory, and equal nature of its fulfillment.

C. According to the above, the law will establish that every Salvadoran must report in a timely manner to the appropriate conscription center. Recruitment will be effected exclusively based on lotteries and registration of volunteers. Military service can be continuous or discontinued.

D. The law mentioned above will contemplate administrative penalties for those who do not fulfill the obligations stipulated therein; it will determine the causes for temporary or permanent absences and the equivalent duties in the various fields of military service and other general provisions.

E. The law will also regulate the armed forces reserves in conformity with Paragraph C of Chapter X of the present agreement.

XII. PREVENTIVE AND PROMOTION MEASURES

Within the context of the objectives of this agreement, the need is recognized to adopt certain measures to promote the better fulfillment of armed forces regulations and to prevent violations of the same. Such measures include the following:

- A. Supervision of armed forces activity by the legislative assembly.
- B. The effective operation of the armed forces inspector general's office. The inspector general will be a member of the armed forces with a spotless background, designated by the president of the republic.
- C. Creation of the armed forces honor tribunal to judge cases which, although not necessarily punishable, attack military honor. This does not preclude the soldiers being brought before justice tribunals.
- D. Reforms to the law to punishes illegal enrichment, expressly including within its jurisdiction the commanders of higher military units and those who hold administrative posts on the same level.
- E. Cancellation of permits to private individuals to carry weapons to be used exclusively by the armed forces and immediate collection of the same.
- F. Dissemination of the armed forces doctrine so that it will be learned by all society.
- G. Adaptation of the armed forces law to make it consistent with the constitutional reforms approved in the April 1991 New York agreement, and the present agreement.

XIII. RELOCATIONS AND DISCHARGES

A. The relocation in the armed forces of the members of those units subject to being eliminated or dissolved will be carried out, provided the relocation is compatible with the number of armed forces troops contemplated in the objectives of this agreement and in the conclusions and recommendations of the *ad hoc* commission set forth in Chapter III.

B. All members discharged in the wake of these agreements will be indemnified with one year's wages. The government will strive to carry out projects to reintegrate them to civilian life.

XIV. INTERNATIONAL VERIFICATION

The United Nations will verify fulfillment of the present agreement with the cooperation of the authorities charged with executing it.

Civil-Military Relations in the Transition to and the Consolidation of Democracy in Latin America

JUAN RIAL
(translated by GABRIEL MARCELLA)

1. From Utopian Socialism to Dictatorships

When Fulgencio Batista fled Havana on 1 January 1959 and gave way to Fidel Castro and his guerrillas, the most important political challenge to twentieth century Latin America appeared. In 1961 Fidel Castro proclaimed his adherence to Marxism-Leninism after a badly mishandled conventional military operation (the 'Bay of Pigs') conducted by the United States failed to dislodge him from power. A year later, the Missile Crisis of 1962 fully introduced the Cold War to Latin America. Yet the the most relevant point about the Cuban Revolution was not its existence on the island next to Florida, but its ability to awaken the socialist utopia in almost all the continent.

In 1961 at the meeting of the Interamerican Social and Economic Council there took place the confrontation between the United States, promoter of the Alliance for Progress and the Peace Corps, and the socialist utopia which considered the Alliance a 'revolution of the latrines' according to Ernesto 'Che' Guevara, who was present at that session. For the first time a great subversive movement focused on the economic, social, and political revolution of the Latin American region, a movement which would acquire continental proportions.

Inspired by the Cuban model, various movements arose. While practically all took inspiration from Marxism-Leninism, they varied in their political interpretations, methods, and strategies for the struggle, their models and international material and ideological supporters, and their endurance and accomplishments. Guevarism with its *foco* concept, fundamentally military and of guerrilla character, inspired various movements, such as Douglas Bravo in Venezuela, those of Lobaton and De la Puente Uceda in Peru, the People's Guerrilla Army and the Uturunco in Argentina. Having a Trotskyist orientation, but also practising Guevarism, were the movements in Guatemala, that of Yon Sosa and part of the work of Revolutionary People's Army of Argentina – the Compania de Monte Rosa Jimenez in Tucuman. Others appeared, some with a syndicalist orientation while others bordered on anarchism, such as: the rural movements of Hugo Blanco and Hector Bejar in Peru or the urban Popular Revolutionary Organisation in Uruguay. Others formed coalitions with socialists of moderate ideology, despite some who took up the armed struggle, such as in Nicaragua where the Sandinistas included personalities like Eden Pastora. In Peru the Shining Path is an example of a Pol Pot type of Maoism combined with social and ethnic resentments.

Some based themselves exclusively in the countryside, like those commanded by Che Guevara in Bolivia. Others had the city as their theatre, such as the Uruguayan movements (Tupamaros and other small groups) and the Argentines (the Montoneros and the major elements of the Revolutionary People's Army). Others combined urban and rural action, such as the Sandinistas, the now legalised M-19 of Colombia and Farabundo Marti in El Salvador, or continue fighting such as the Shining Path.

In the 1960s the dominant form was the guerrilla movement, basically rural, in Argentina, Bolivia, Brasil, Guatemala, Peru and Venezuela. All were defeated. Only the Colombian subversive movements sustained themselves as guerrilla combatants and even here they inherited the violence begun in the 1940s. In Guatemala they remained latent and reappeared in the 1970s. Towards the end of the 1960s and at the beginning of the 1970s there appeared movements that practise a mixture of armed propaganda and terrorism in the urban centres of Argentina, Brazil, Chile, and Uruguay. All were defeated. In Nicaragua the Sandinistas operated openly as an insurrectionist movement and become the second to triumph in Latin America, in 1979. In the 1980s the Farabundo Marti movement appeared with strength in El Salvador. These insurgents survived and were integrated into the political process with some difficulty. In Peru the Shining Path appeared exactly during the period of redemocratisation. In Colombia peace accords were struck with elements of the guerrilla movements, the most significant being the April 19, while others continue their struggle. In Guatemala, also after redemocratisation, a peace accord is sought with the guerrilla movements grouped into the UNRG – the Guatemalan National Guerrilla Movement.[1]

Between the Cuban Revolution and 1962 there were efforts at guerrilla resistance, but these were eventually defeated. With the triumph of the Sandinistas the 'contras' appeared in 1981. The latter ultimately disbanded when the opposition won electorally in 1990. Yet there also appeared new forms of violent action associated with the refinement and distribution of narcotics. Their subversive potential is not tied to an ideological line nor posited on combating the prevailing socio-economic system. It is, rather, tied to groups organised as 'mafias' who seek a position of recognised power in society.

Some groups engaged in armed warfare in the form of guerrilla action or armed propaganda or terrorism, a perverse variant, as their principal form of violent action. Others engage in such criminal activities as robbery, kidnappings for extortion, for example. Rarely do they 'liberate' territory or establish embryonic military forces.

All these actions were resisted by the states and by their military and security forces. The destruction of the old Cuban guard that defended the Batista government in 1959 and the execution of its leaders provoked a growing fear in the local military institutions.[2] The conviction among leaders of political parties that they could not handle these situations and the tendency of militaries to intervene constantly in political affairs,[3] led military institutions in the majority of countries from the 1970s to the early 1980s to establish dictatorships in almost the entire region.[4]

Some of the models of dictatorship in which the armed forces participated attempted to re-establish society. The successful example, as seen from the perspective of 1992, was the Chilean.[5] Especially since 1982, Chile has mounted a neoliberal economic and social experiment which, after the transition to democracy in 1989, has been maintained by the democratic government. Another successful experience was the Brazilian one begun in 1964. In the 1970s it was considered an 'economic miracle' given the sustained growth of Brazilian industry and the rapid process of modernisation that the country entered.[6] While the 1980s saw the establishment of the model of an open economy in the aftermath of the regional crisis brought about by the foreign debt[7], the Brazilian model came to be considered a failure. Yet this is a view after the fact that fails to take into account the profound transformation which Brazil had before the mid-1980s.

In Peru the military led by a *caudillo* chose a statist authoritarian developmental model, with certain socialist aspects. The seven-year period of General Velasco Alvarado did not produce sustained development, despite the process of modernisation that he intoduced. The military institution decided to end the experiment in 1975. Another effort which might be considered 'leftist' was that of the Civil-Military Junta of El Salvador in 1978, which lasted for a brief time.

In the majority of the remaining cases, even though the phraseology announced new times, such as the 'Argentine Revolution' of 1966, the military institution supported the dictatorships which, though strongly repressive, had no other objective but to exercise a commissarial 'dictatorship' according to the terminology of Carl Schmitt. Such a scheme exercised 'moderating' power between contenders which, at the end, would lead to restoration of political stability.[8] The military attempted to exercise violence in a conservative manner and not in a manner designed to restructure society,[9] despite the fact that often the rhetoric spoke of a 'new order' and even of 'revolution'.

FIGURE 1

FORMS OF DICTATORSHIP

Type of dictatorship →	Moderating	Restructuring	Traditional
Societal model ↓			
Socialist		Cuba 1959 Nicaragua 1979–84	

Statist market	Argentina 1970–73
	Bolivia (regimes of
	  Barrientos, Ovando,
	  Banzer)
	Brazil 1964–68, 1982–85
	Guatemala
	Honduras
	Peru 1975–79
	Uruguay 1973–74
		Brazil 1968
		Ecuador 1972–78	

Statist market with
  tendency toward
  fiscal and
  commercial
  liberalisation
	Argentina 1966–70,
	  1976–82
	Chile 1973–78
	El Salvador 1978–82
	Uruguay 1974–84		

Neoliberal		Chile 1978–89	

Patrimonial			Bolivia (criminal
			  regime of Garcia
			  Meza)
			Dominican Rep.
			  of Trujillo
			Haiti
			Nicaragua to 1979
			Panama (Noriega)
			Paraguay until 1989

In Figure 1 we have summarised the types of dictatorial government according to its dominant form and its model of society. A moderating dictatorship seeks to simply eliminate the existing conflict in order to separate the contenders for power. The basic idea is to return government to the normal pre-existing system, retaining the reforms in order to avoid falling back into what they perceived to be the causes of the original crisis that brought on the dictatorship. The restructuring or structuring model implies an attempt to create a substantial change in society, breaking with the past. We call a traditional dictatorship one which rules in disarticulated countries or where the task of building a nation and the processes of modernisation are slow. Here those who control the military are those who run the country, often in connivance with a local oligarchy. Normally the military is very primitive and does not qualify as a military force.

With respect to the societal models, we have in mind the socialist option, including Nicaragua more for its goals than for its achievements. We consider it a dictatorship by the way it acceded to power, despite not having proclaimed it, like it was done in Cuba. We call 'socialistic' the case of Peru under General Velasco Alvarado and the failed attempt of the Salvadoran Junta of 1978 because, even if they did not proclaim the socialist objective, their orientation tended in that direction.

The patrimonialist styles belong to the traditional dictatorships. These lack a modern socio-economic model, they confuse private interests of the dominant sectors with the public interest.

We distinguish three levels of models of market economies. One is statist, based on the productive efforts of the state during the twentieth century in the entire region, which make it the guide of the social and economic processes by means of development styles that emphasise assistance in the social arena and 'dirigisme', regulatory control of the economy. A variant of this is one that permits certain levels of liberalisation, considerably in the financial area and less in the commercial. The third type, which might be viewed a different model, is the deregulating state in the social and economic spheres – the 'neoliberal'.

FIGURE 2

FORMS OF REPRESSION

Intimidation	Societal Patrol	Social Control	Populist Praetorianism
Argentina	Bolivia (except 1st	Cuba	Bolivia (in periods
Bolivia (1st Banzer	phase of Banzer &	Nicaragua	of Barrientos &
govt.)	certain periods of	Panama (final part	Ovando & later
Brazil (parts of	Barrientos &	Noriega regime)	Torres)
Costa e Silva &	Ovando)	Peru, 1968–75	Ecuador
Garrastazu govts.)	Brazil (all other times)		Haiti
Chile (initial period	Chile (all other times)		Panama
& 1982–83)	Honduras		Paraguay
El Salvador			
Guatemala			
Uruguay			

There is no relationship between forms of dictatorship and the models they espoused with the styles of repression employed by each one of them, but tendencies can be seen. Those orientated towards a socialist model tended to construct systems of social integration. Going from the police-style committees for the Defence of the Revolution in Cuba, to the effort to create the National Mobilisation System in Velasco Alvarado's Peru, to the incipient experience of Noriega in creating the Panamanian Dignity Battalions, all the repression aspired to the same end. Through either persuasion, fear or intimidation, the effort was to establish positive support for the regime.

The patrimonial regimes tended towards a populist campaign of repression, favouring sectors of the population, such as the Colorado Party and its clientelist network in Paraguay, or those tied to the Ton Ton Macoutes in Haiti. Others, such as the Ecuadoran, should not really be considered repressive despite being dictatorships.

The moderate or restructuring regimes, with either statist or market economic models, oscillated between 'patrolling or constant vigilance' over society. This meant at the same time firm repression of distinct opposition groups: the hardline model imposed control through fear. The constant conduct of persecution and the subjection to pressures of social sectors, not with the objective of persuading or integrating them, but of forcing them to obey, combined with the spreading through rumour of atrocities or tough punishment received by enemies, characterised various regimes.

2. The Transitions[10]

The Peruvian dictatorship was among the first to open the way for the new wave of democracy in the region. In 1975 the seven-year period of Velasco Alvarado and his semi-socialist experience ended. From then until 1979 the military conducted a political opening which permitted a return to the status quo. It was done through a constituent assembly that approved a basic charter and through an election which brought to the presidency the same person who was unceremoniously removed from the Pizarro Palace in 1968, the architect Fernando Belaunde Terry.[11]

In Ecuador the military government ended at the same time. Thanks to the petroleum boom, it modernised the country, especially the region around Quito. It also created a middle class linked to this statist effort. With these objectives achieved and in order to avoid internal dissent, the military also stimulated a transition. A constituent assembly opened the process which adjusted the election to allow the military and its allies to prevent the coming to power of the populist Assad Bucaram.[12]

In the countries of the Southern Cone, the Uruguayan dictatorship fell apart after their plan of constitutional reform failed popular approval in 1980. This produced internal divisions within the military. The Argentine military committed the error of undertaking a limited military adventure in the Malvinas/Falklands, after having attempted a more serious one with Chile, which was aborted in 1978.[14] At the same time the two attempts at restructuring the socio-economic system into an open one were limited to the financial, and on a lesser scale, to the commercial area.

The end of the Brazilian miracle coincided with the political opening promoted by the presidents Generals Geisel and Figuereido. The long transition culminated in 1985. The military thought the country was headed in the right direction and that they should look after their professional concerns, thereby avoiding internal divisions. They took into account that their attempt to convert Brazil into an intermediate power and their special relationship with the United States forced them to change the political system. They wanted this to be a controlled change, thus the prudent steps and the resistance to pressures for a more rapid democratisation process. They rejected the demand for direct presidential elections in 1984–85.

In Paraguay the patrimonialist dictatorship of Alfredo Stroessner ended in 1989. His colleagues in the armed forces, headed by the father-in-law of his son, General Andres Rodriguez, and encouraged by younger officers, felt uncomfortable in the midst of a clientelist regime founded on illegal activities. They wanted to keep the military, but with a new foundation linked to the the new interests emerging from the modernisation of the country, among them the services tied to the energy sector and to the new crops being cultivated in the central corridor of the country.

Chile was the successful example. The technocratic alliance with the government of General Augusto Pinochet stimulated substantial change in the country. Chile's democratic tradition, the international pressures and the negative image of the country acquired in 1973 with the bombardment of 'La Moneda' (the presidential palace) and the death of President Salvador Allende, combined to defeat the attempt to continue the regime in the elections of 1988. But only partly so. A conservative political force has formed to ensure the continuation of the socio-economic structure. The winning alliance in the elections of 1989 had to follow this path. At the same time, General Pinochet placed himself as the guarantor of this system's continuity by remaining as commander of the Army.

Venezuela and Colombia were the only South American countries which kept institutional continuity in the entire period that followed the

Cuban Revolution. The defeat of the Venezuelan guerrillas in the early 1960s was carried out within the framework of democratic principles.

Colombia is a country which could hardly be considered a model of stability. In the face of continued urban and rural guerrilla violence of various types, the military did not assume the daily control of national politics. It is a country of strong regional differences and diffuse powers which did not produce a civilian coalition to unite with the military to form a moderating power. Later, in the 1980s, came the violence of the narcotraffickers which sought for their wealth political power and social recognition. Within this process Colombia attempted to widen the democratic base by creating new means for local political participation – direct popular election of mayors and reform of the constitution.

In Central America two cases of democratic transition occurred. They were certainly precarious in the context of warfare: Nicaragua in 1990 and previously El Salvador in 1985. In both cases the pressure of the United States was very significant in getting results. At the end of 1991 and early in 1992 El Salvador reached new peace accords, while in Nicaragua the internal war ended with the triumph of Violeta Chamorro in the elections of 1990.

Guatemala's transition also began in 1985 and slightly before that in Honduras. Panama is a very special case because the Noriega regime ended as the result of the invasion by the forces of the United States at the end of 1989.

The attemps to undertake a transition in Haiti after the fall of the Duvalier family have until now failed. Cuba continues to be a socialist country with a bureaucratic dictatorship. The Dominican Republic had no breaks of institutional order after the rebellion of Colonel Caamaño in 1965 and the intervention of the Organization of American States. Even here the electoral process has always been difficult.

3. The Transitions and the Processes of Redemocratisation

In the negotiated transitions normally the armed forces tried to achieve not only an orderly transfer of power, but also to reserve political power for themselves or, at least, a strong institutional autonomy.[16] This was the case in Brazil, Uruguay, and Chile. Those forces that did not achieve this, such as the Argentine, faced enormous difficulties in the form of rebellions. In Central America the transitions were more complex and had a greater international involvement, especially the United States.

At first it was thought that the power of the armed forces to influence the political systems would be very high. However, by 1989, with the collapse of the socialist world Latin America entered a new environment which rapidly eroded the political power of the military institutions throughout the region. As we have indicated elsewhere the very concept of Latin America appears difficult to retain for all practical effect. The distinction between Central America, the Caribbean, the Andean world, the Southern Cone (with the exception of Chile, which follows its own path), and Brazil makes it necessary to take into account the distinctiveness of each rather than arrive at a common analysis for the entire region.

Some of the academic studies spoke of the special democratic forms[17] or of processes that led to electing governments democratically, but not to establishing representative democratic institutions.[18] Nonetheless, and despite the fragility of the institutions, forms of civilian government have been maintained, many of them product of new ways of conducting politics that led to the proliferation of 'new caudillos'[19] supported by a new politics brought on by a process of downsizing the state. The armed forces, a significant part of the state apparatus, have not escaped this process.

The armed forces retained the most political power in Chile. Here they assured themselves on the one hand institutional autonomy, which meant maintaining the system of traditional corporate values, a concept of medieval origin, the norms that guide and control the military career, the formation of the officer corps and some control over the budget that the armed forces receive.

At the same time a large guarantee was added: General Augusto Pinochet would stay in command of the most important service while it was made clear that there would be no investigations of the past or of the conduct of the armed forces. It was also implied that there would be no going back in the socio-economic and political model and that any profound change in the path taken would be vetoed. Up to 1992 the situation has not changed much, except for the real collapse of socialism which has forced a renewal that even Pinochet favours in order to meet the foreign pressures (see further discussion on this point in succeeding pages).

In other countries, such as Brazil, the armed force initially tried to achieve a similar situation. In Brazil the military resisted the establishment of a Ministry of Defence, but military power has been reduced by the external pressures which eroded their attempts at technological development and also by the rapid decline of the defence budget.

The Uruguayan military successfully resisted an effort to judge the past. They were able to do so because of the support of the civilian political leadership, thereby avoiding a confrontation that might have brought serious and uncertain consequences. Yet they also lost power quickly, especially with the reduction of the defence budget.

The Paraguayan military still have significant power. They are involved in internal struggles which have to do with the Colorado Party who holds on to the government in 1993.

The military lost position in Argentina, despite consecutive rebellions headed first by Aldo Rico and later by Mohamed A. Seineldin. The rebellions caused serious problems for the government, especially that of Dr Raul Alfonsin which conducted an erratic and somewhat unrealistic policy over this matter. Putting down the rebellions, combined with the foreign pressures and the drastic reduction of the budget placed the military institution in a state of decomposition from which it has not recovered.[20] In 1992–93 the Argentine military's situation became more hopeful with the establishment of new professional norms, new military strategy, and a modern educational system for officers and non-commissioned officers. Additionally, Argentina has participated in a major way in UN peacekeeping in the former Yugoslavia.

The Peruvian military has gone through a similar process, the result of the lack of leadership, small budget, the corrosive effect of the corruption linked to the cultivation and marketing of drugs, and of the inability to deal with a subversive political movement with limited military capability, which is the Shining Path. Bolivia is similar, despite the absence of a strong subversive movement.

In Ecuador the military continued to maintain their distance from daily political decisions. Yet, they tried to accumulate and control resources in order to avoid falling into the poverty that affects the other militaries of the region.

In Venezuela, where there was no transition to democracy and where institutional continuity was maintained, there was a serious deterioration in the military institution. In early 1992 Lieutenant Colonel Hugo Chavez Frias led a rebellion by middle grade officers. This insurrection was followed by another in November 1992 and the dismissal of the elected President Carlos Andres Perez by the Congress. The Venezuelan civilian and military leadership thus faced the task of restoring discipline and professionalism to the military ranks.

In Panama the American invasion of December 1989 terminated the Panamanian Defense Forces, leaving Panama without a military force. The new problem became establishing an effective and credible police force.

In Nicaragua the Sandinistas had negotiated the permanence of their armed forces in exchange for reductions in troop strength and budget. They furthermore accepted the changing of the 'revolutionary' and partisan police into a national force. This process is still underway.

In Guatemala the military maintain a greater capacity of political veto and control enough resources to allow a certain autonomy. Honduras is affected by the end of its role as a base of operations for the Contras and by the reduction of the budget. The Salvadorean military are in a process of restructuring as the result of the Peace Accords and find it difficult to exercise political power.

In summary, there are cases of strong political power held by the military. It is the case in Chile through the presence of General Pinochet, to which is added, paradoxically, the economic success of the country which sustains the flow of important resources to the military. In Paraguay it is because the process of transition is not complete. In Guatemala it is the continuing confrontation with subversive groups while in Brazil it is for a more marked reason – the fear of a vacuum of power.

In the other cases the prevailing situation indicates that the military is not a relevant political actor that conditions the political conduct of governments. In some countries the military retain greater corporate autonomy, meaning the handling of money and authority to resolve internally the issues of organisation and institutional values. In others, the budgetary scarcity combined with the loss of public image, brings them to an existential crisis.[21] This implies internal problems in a force that loses motivation, finds itself disorientated in terms of its professional function and the absence of resources. It translated into problems of recruiting new members to the officer corps with the quality adequate for the task and career. This could in the future lead to episodes of passive or active indiscipline,[22] as well as taking on a low profile in the corporate interest.

This situation leads to institutional hypothermia.[23] The senior officer corps will attempt to reduce to a minimum their professional activities and allow the institution to survive until a more favourable opportunity arises in the future. In some cases the officers will not be able to control their subordinates sufficiently, such as occurred in Bolivia and Peru where the effort to eliminate the production and marketing of drugs led to the corruption of the middle ranks. Similarly, it could lead to the situation that occurred in Venezuela, where the discontent within the middle ranks led to revolt in 1992, or to the situation in the Dominican Republic, where the wholly professional military, because of few resources, has hardly any confidence in its professionalism.

4. Civil-Military Relations

The relations between the armed forces and the governments and, more generally the political system at the beginning, assumed the form, in almost all the countries, of the accommodation of elites.[24] This was a negotiation between members of the military leadership and a small part of the political elite responsible for taking decisions about the resources to be allocated to the military, the promotions of senior officers and everything that affected the performance of the military institution. In its initial stages the situation was one of passive support to the democratic regime, one of lack of confidence in a regime they believed weak and furthermore responsible for the success of the subversives or for the national disorganisation that took place in the recent past. Therefore they practised a 'negative integration' with the government they were supposed to serve. They supported the process of restoration or building democracy in practice, but their rhetoric tended to support the superiority or the authoritarian experience.

The substantive theme of the discussion in this accommodation has been the level of autonomy which the military maintains. In some cases the subordination of the military to political authority has evolved. In Cuba subordination via ideological party control is maintained. Ecuador comes close to 'objective' subordination, a concept which means converting the military to an autonomous professional institution with no political role, much as Argentina is attempting to do. In the case of Ecuador there might be uncertainty about this type of control, given the fact that it could be termed 'subjective' control because the military has assured itself mechanisms for survival independent of the direction of daily political affairs.[25] Some other countries exercise subjective control through the mechanism of appointing military commanders in whom the state has confidence.[26]

In two states relations are tense. Nicaragua, the scene of frequent clashes, after the election of 1990 has been in constant negotiation between the military leadership and the government. The military wants to survive and keep its autonomy. The government wants to reduce it. For the moment, neither side has been able to impose itself and the balance is precarious.[27] The other case of tense relations is Chile, where Augusto Pinochet (who is 78 years of age, while the next senior general is 55 years of age) conditions the policy of the government. Efforts to remove him have failed.

In Paraguay civil-military relations do not exactly exist. There is such a strong interconnection between the government and the military that

it is difficult to distinguish the military institution from the structure of
power.

FIGURE 3

CIVIL-MILITARY RELATIONS IN 1993

Accommodation of elites	Bolivia, Brazil, El Salvador, Guatemala, Honduras
Subjective subordination via designation of leaders of confidence	Argentina,* Colombia, Dominican Republic, Peru, Uruguay, Venezuela
Subordination which combines 'subjectivity' via institutionalised norms with 'professional objective'[29] control	Ecuador
Subordination via ideology-party	Cuba
Tense relations	Chile, Nicaragua
Military-government mix	Paraguay

*Could be moving towards a form of objective subordination.

5. The 'New International Order'[30] Evolving and the Military

The new order that is developing and constantly changing has perplexed
the military leaders of Latin America. The majority of them command
military organisations which are very traditional in nature, weakly
related to the economy of the country they are to serve.[31] The triumph
of market capitalism which tends toward a strong deregulation has
substantially reduced the influence of the state. This fact creates
confusion in the military institution, because the triumph against
communism takes shape within a context that the military does not
perceive as adequate. The triumph of capitalism and of the market
economy happens at the cost of the loss of power by the state, of the
organism which controls society. This process weakens the military
because it is part of the state system that privatises and deregulates an
important number of its activities. For those armed forces which do not
have confidence in the market economy,[32] since the values of the market
are very far from the medieval values of the military, this point makes
them take a timid attitude towards the facts which are shaping the new
system of international relations.[33] Herbert Spencer indicated in his
Principles of Sociology[34] that industrial society was incompatible with
the military warrior. The incorporation of modern industrial technology
into warfare or its threat may indeed have changed these calculations. It
is important to keep in mind that capitalism has a universal tendency to
market every relationship, to break the traditional relationship between
the military and the social and political community. This in turn impedes

the consolidation of strong corporate organisations such as the traditional military, pushing them to take on lighter forms, based on the occupational model[35] and complemented by the formation of elites. These may tend to have the value system of the mercenary.

The fall of real socialism, besides making it possible to lose the enemy easily identifiable as the 'international communist', has had the effect of introducing greater confusion. Despite the disappearance of the Soviet Union, subversive movements survive and may acquire new forms, putting to rest the simplistic analysis that stated that the existence of these movements depended upon foreign assistance. It is true that a great part of the strength of these movements in the 1960s and 1970s was due to the indirect confrontation between the two superpowers. Once the confrontation disappeared there remained the state and the prevailing socio-economic system as targets.

In this evolving international order new problems arise that were not anticipated by the armed forces at the time of redemocratisation. For the military of the most important countries of the region the level of pressures against the development of weapons of mass destruction and of high technology increase.[36] With this, even if they overcome their economic problems and then have the resources, neither Argentina nor Brazil have the capacity to reach the levels of the first world.

At another level there is constant pressure to reduce the number of available forces as well their costs. The international organisations that scrutinise and try to control these developments exercise pressure, which will probably increase, in order to make such measures effective.

The advanced countries seek to reduce the forces of the smaller countries so that they become a 'national guard' or a 'gendarmerie', even though they still may be called armies. Their mission is to take care of internal order, in addition to maritime and air services, to be adequate for such tasks as transport, rescue, emergency support, and securing the air and maritime space. In summary: that they comprise forces for special security, but not a military force. Emphasis would be on performing non-military tasks, such as the work of the corps of engineers, or to provide medical assistance with medical teams or military nurses, or the task of colonising the forest or protecting the environment. This indicates that the task of the traditional military is in question or is not considered relevant. In other cases the abolition of the symbols of a military force is advocated, as is taking place in Panama.

In the meantime, some militaries see participation in international peacekeeping forces as a momentary outlet for their problems. Whereas for the governments this is a way of gaining influence with the dominant powers, for the military leaderships it is a way of demonstrating their utility and of keeping their personnel motivated. For those troops who take part, especially among the lower ranks, it is a way of earning significant income.[37] They constitute labour that is cheaper than that available among the countries of the first world, whose motivation for the assignment is purely professional, devoid of any other significance. At the same time, peacekeeping permits the poor forces of these countries to undertake an important professional exercise, at a very low risk.

The reaction to external pressures has been swift. In various speeches the chiefs of armed forces of the region have expressed displeasure with the United States. At times they mention the drug war exclusively, but at other times they go beyond this. The most important movement of this type is headed by General Augusto Pinochet, who seeks to create a viable alternative for the military of his country and those of potential allies in the context of an unfavourable international situation.[38]

In view of these problems and the growing budget cuts, the militaries face threats. The principal one is not having clear what is real and what is a ghost of the past, or of a plausible future, or what is important enough to merit priority attention, given the scarce resources available, and precisely how should these threats be faced.

The ghost of nationalism which has strongly re-emerged in this evolving new world order has placed in doubt the stability of borders, despite the fact that the majority of global conflicts appear to be solved, or on the way to being so,[39] and given the agreements recently made in the region.[40]

Other problems appear for now to have only the character of internal agitation by tiny groups, at times united in the search for a new Utopia: such as the indigenist, which establish their unity among groups that are based on ethnic criteria. The weakness of the nation state in some countries favours the growth of this problem.[41]

Subversion against the state and the socio-economic system is still a threat, regardless of the fall of the socialist Utopia. Some continue to carry the banner,[42] but this can be substituted by other Utopias or by more primitive emotional motivation, such as the above-mentioned ethnic one.

The control of internal order against popular uprising is an ever present task, a type of support given to police incapable of handling the problem. With economic crisis, constant adjustments and growing political inequality it appears that this will be a routine task. Yet it can also lead the military into a new cycle of support for populist dictatorships along the lines of Velazco in Peru's recent history.[43]

With respect to the tasks created by the illegal trade in drugs it is purely a support role to the police, of the result of the need to fight subversive groups that thrive on the income produced by this activity.[44] With reason the majority of the armed forces of the region tries to avoid becoming involved in such activities. These activities corrupt personnel, they are a police responsibility, not military, and most importantly, do not lead the military to success. However, it seems difficult for some countries of the region to avoid the pressures of the United States to continue in the effort. Obviously, the form may be filled but the results will be disappointing.[45]

FIGURE 4

THREATS WHICH THE MILITARY MIGHT FACE

Political and/or social subversion.	Bolivia,* Colombia, Ecuador,* Guatemala, Panama,* Peru
Clashes with drug cartels which seek to destabilise the state to consolidate their 'mafia' corporate power.**	Colombia
Support police efforts to eradicate plantings and laboratories stemming from international pressures.	Bolivia, Colombia, Peru
Clashes with alliances of subversives and drug traffickers.	Peru
Problems stemming adjustments to the peace process; clashes with groups that resist the accords.	Nicaragua, El Salvador, possibly in Guatemala, Colombia in future
Posible emergence of ethnic problems, combining with agitation of class inequalities.	Future problems possible in Bolivia, Ecuador, Guatemala, Peru
Support to police in case of popular uprisings caused principally by economic problems.	Practically includes all countries

Notes: *Incipient actions which could disappear or increase in the short term, depending on the comprehensive handling of the political dituation. In the Chilean case isolated incidents of minor significance occur.
**Refers to movements which accept the prevailing socio-economic system, the market, even though they behave in a violent and corrupt way. With respect to the state they seek to avoid it or to manipulate it according to their interests.

The possibilities of conventional conflicts between states, even though they may be perceived by the military institutions, are not considered here. These confrontations may be conceived as threats from the professional military perspective but, for political reasons, they do not appear to have the possibility of becoming threats that lead to the outbreak of hostilities. Nonetheless, their very possibility will always be used by some military institutions in order to obtain equipment and resources. The concept of deterrence will always be present in a military as long as the existence of the national state is considered the principal institution organising the international system.

New economic blocs are developing as well as multinational businesses which are more powerful than any small state of the region. It is difficult to understand which threat, if there is one, this implies, but the armed forces are beginning to perceive the dangers that economic blocs constitute. Sub-regional blocs such as MERCOSUR (Argentina, Brazil, Uruguay, Paraguay) caused some concerns among the respective military staffs of the member countries. They see it as an opportunity to strengthen ties among the militaries. The small countries regard it as a chance to obtain equipment while the large ones it as a chance to sell. Yet the issue is latent and addresses one of the most difficult points upon which have foundered all efforts at economic integration: the symbolic plane.

In the face of an international system of blocs the military corporations of South America wish to maintain a good substantive relationship with the United States, the principal world power, despite the overload this produces for the principal 'guarantor' of the new world order.[46] However, at the same time the militaries will try to keep other supports: in Europe or Israel, and on a lesser scale Taiwan, in order to keep a counterweight against the 'hegemonic' presence of the United States.

6. Civil-Military Relations in the New Context

With the availability of new ways of conducting politics through the communications media, the armed forces of each country have a new support for their political activities. If the elected president survives the military will support him even though he may have violated the constitution, as happened with Alberto Fujimori in Peru. They will shun a *coup d'état* which would render them protagonists. Their recent experience, combined with the absence of local support (there are no business or international groups, traditional business or governments, that might want to support them), suggests that this danger will not materialise. However, other than the *caudillo* example (Fujimori) of the handling of the military, we cannot find strong institutional structures for civil-military relations.

As is traditional, there are no civilian elites that manage military and defence issues. The handling of these responsibilities brings no political profit. There are no industrial complexes and important social questions that are part of military and defence problems. To the contrary, the filling of positions in the ministries of defence is considered marginal to a career and is a heavy responsibility for a civilian. Certainly there are few that are qualified for them and, generally speaking, they would not be easily accepted either by political or by military leaders.[47]

Among the militaries that practice hypothermia as a means of survival the important thing is to participate in the process of reconstruction and the accommodation to the new scenarios in order to avoid negative consequences. The principal one would be the possible elimination of the armed forces, a result favoured by corruption and generalised inefficiency. This scenario compromises the future of the military because it introduces the loss of motivation among ther current and future members. If this occurs and the military survives, it will tend to turn it 'mercenary' and there could occur frequent episodes of covert and open indiscipline. In this last scenario the extreme would be the appearance of 'warlords', an outcome that must be avoided.

To come to grips with a programme of reconstitution of the armed forces we need, in principle, to define clearly whether we desire to have them. This implies engaging all of society and the civilian elites. We believe the answer should be yes. After we accept this premise we need to define its purpose. This should be military rather than having a force with a military appearance performing non-military functions. Last, we need to discuss what resources it should have and therefore how should it be organised, trained, and deployed.

This agenda appears remote to the majority of countries, where the civilian elite feels secure about coups and handles the issue according to other considerations, such as using the military only as an instrument for maintaining internal order, as an auxiliary police. If indeed currently there are no serious problems, it would be well to keep thinking about this issue, so that we avoid unforeseen surprises. The effort undertaken by various civilian and military groups to protect the process of democratic transition and consolidation no longer enjoys the support it had during the mid-1980s. We believe it would be shortsighted to jettison the work already accumulated and return to the *status quo ante* in the near future. We may face an unpleasant outcome based on the conclusions of this essay.

NOTES

1. See Timothy P. Wickam Crowley, *Guerrillas and Revolution in Latin America* (Princeton: Princeton UP, 1990); James Kohl and John Litt, *Urban Guerrilla Warfare in Latin America* (Cambridge, MA: MIT, 1974).
2. We exclude Mexico from our entire analysis. The unique elements of its political system, which until recently had only one relevant party, combined with its border

status with the United States, gives the country a very special category, which, from the situation of 1992 makes us exclude it from the analysis that follows. Furthermore, we reiterate that Latin America is an elusive concept, because the differences between regions and countries are very distinct. See Juan Rial, 'Las Fuerzas Armadas y la cuestion de la democracia en America Latina', in Louis W. Goodman, Johanna S.R. Mendelson and Juan Rial (eds.), *Los militares y la democracia* (Montevideo: Peitho, 1990).

3. See, among others, Genaro Arriagada, *El Pensamiento politico de los militares* (Santiago: CISEC, 1981); Morris Janowitz and Jacques Van Doorn (eds.), *On Military Intervention* (Rotterdam: Rotterdam University Press 1971); Alain Rouquie, *El estado militar en America Latina* (Mexico: Siglo XXI, 1984); Augusto Varas (ed.), *La autonomia militar en America Latina* (Caracas: Nueva Sociedad, 1988).

4. Guillermo O'Donnell speaks of the age of bureaucratic–authoritarian regimes to refer to the political formulas that appeared at that time, independent of their formation and not as military dictatorships. See *El estado burocratico-autoritario, 1966–1973. Triunfo, Derrotas y Crisis* (Buenos Aires: Editorial Belgrano, 1982); see also David Collier (ed.), *The New Authoritarianism in Latin America* (Princeton, NJ: Princeton UP, 1979); and Juan Linz and Alfred Stepan (eds.), *The Breakdown of Democratic Regimes* (Baltimore: Johns Hopkins UP, 1978).

5. See Manuel A. Garreton, *El proceso politico chileno* (Santiago: FLACSO, 1983) and *Dictaduras y democratizacion*, (Santiago FLACSO, 1984); Arturo and Samuel Valenzuela (eds.), *Military Rule in Chile: Dictatorship and Opposition* (Baltimore: Johns Hopkins UP, 1986).

6. See Alfred Stepan (ed.), *Authoritarian Brazil* (New Haven, CT: Yale UP, 1973).

7. See Rosemary Thorp and Laurence Whitehead (eds.), *Inflation and Stabilization in Latin America: Latin American Debt and the Adjustment Crisis* (London: Macmillan Press, 1987).

8. Carl Schmitt, *La Dictadura* (Madrid: Rensto de Occidente, 1968), trans. of *Die Diktatur* (Berlin: Duncker & Humbloy, 1964). See Juan Rial, 'Transitions in Latin America on the Threshold of the 1990s', *International Social Science Journal*, No. 128 (May 1991).

9. See Walter Benjamin, *Para una critica de la violencia* (Mexico: Premia, 1982).

10. In general see Enrique Baloyra (ed.), *Comparing New Democracies: Transition and Consolidation in Mediterranean Europe and Southern Cone* (Boulder, CO: Westview, 1987); Larry Diamond, Juan Linz, and Seymour M. Lipset, *Democracy in Developing Countries*, Vol. 4 (Boulder, CO: Lynne Rienner, 1989); Pedro Nikken (ed.), *Agenda para la consolidacion de la Democracia* (San José, Costa Rica: IIDH/CAPEL, 1990); Leonardo Morlino, *Come Cambiano i Regimi Politici: Strumenti di Analisi* (Milano: Ranco Angeli, 1980); Guillermo O'Donnell, Philippe Schmitter, and Lawrence Whitehead, *Transitions from Authoritarian Rule* (Baltimore: Johns Hopkins UP, 1986); Robert Pastor, *Democracy in the Americas* (NY: Holmes & Meier, 1989); Philippe Schmitter, 'Speculations About the Prospective Demise of Authoritarian Regimes and its Possible Consequences', *Wilson Center Working Papers*, No.60, 1979 and the two special numbers of the *International Social Science Journal*, Nos.128 and 129, 'The Age of Democracy' and 'Rethinking Democracy', pub. in 1991. The book by O'Donnell *et al.*, includes the work of Alain Rouquie, 'Demilitarization and the Institutionalization of Military-Dominated Polties in Latin America', pp.108–36.

11. See Alfred Stepan, *State and Society: Peru in Comparative Perspective*, (Princeton, NJ: Princeton UP, 1978).

12. See Osvaldo Hurtado, *El poder politico en Ecuador*, 3rd ed. (Quito: Universidad Catolica, 1979).

13. See Juan Rial, 'Transicion hacia la democracia y restauracion en el Uruguay, 1985–1989', in Nikken (ed.), *Agenda para la consolidacion de la democracia en America Latina*; and in *Peitho, Documentos de Trabajo*, No.46, (Montevideo, 1990).

14. Juan Corradi, *The Fitful Republic* (Boulder, CO: Westview, 1985); Carlos Floria, La turbulenta transicion de la Argentina secreta', in Nikken, *Agenda para la consolida-*

cion de la democracia en America Latina; José Nun and Juan Carlos Portantiero (eds.), *Ensayos sobre la transicion democratica en la Argentina* (Buenos Aires: Punto Sur, 1987); Oscar Oszlak, editor, *'Proceso', crisis y transicion democratica*, 2 vols. (Buenos Aires: Ceal, 1984).

15. See Bolivar Lamounier, *Partidos e Utopias: O Brasil no Limiar dos Anos 90*, (São Paulo: Loyola, 1989); Fabio Wanderley Reis and Guillermo O'Donnell (eds.), *A Democracia no Brasil. Dilemas e perspectivas* (São Paulo: Vertice, 1988).

16. In this case not only to maintain a high professional level 'uncontaminated by political pressures', but also to maintain itself as an institutional reserve in case of a new crisis of the state and the political regime.

17. Terry Karl and Philippe Schmitter, 'Modes of Transition in Latin America, Southern Europe, and Eastern Europe', in *International Social Science Journal*, No. 128, May 1991.

18. See Guillermo O'Donnell, 'Delegative Democracy', draft of the meeting 'East and South System Transformation', place unknown, Dec. 1990.

19. See Carina Perelli, 'Backwards into the Future: The New Caudillos in the Framework of the Retreat of the State in South America', in *Peitho, Documentos de Trabajo* No. 84 (Montevideo, 1992).

20. There are various proposals to re-establish confidence in the armed forces. See, e.g, Virgilio Beltran, 'Marco general para el estudio de la reorganizacion del Ejercito', Draft, mimeo, Buenos Aires, 1991.

21. Brazilian Adm. Ferreira Vidigal used this expression in various seminars conducted on the subject in the region.

22. We refer to the lack of interest for the profession, and for the protection of personnel under their command, which makes the military lose cohesion and quality as an instrument that can utilise the threat of and use of force efficiently.

23. This concept was expressed orally by Richard Millett in a seminar held at Washington DC in 1992.

24. See Alfred Stepan, *Rethinking Military Politics: Brazil and the Southern Cone* (Princeton, NJ: Princeton University Press, 1988). Stepan has used this concept of accommodation on numerous occasions, to signify a constant negotiation between the military elite and the civilian elite.

25. The military possesses a fixed percentage of the petroleum revenues to apply to the modernisation and maintenance of its equipment, it manages commercial enterprises and a financial institution to meet the social security needs of retired personnel.

26. See Samuel Huntington, *The Soldier and the State* (Cambridge, MA: Harvard UP, 1957), for the concepts of 'objective' and 'subjective' control.

27. From the symbolic point of view the principal political operator of the government, Antonio Lacayo, seeks to to replace Gen. Humberto Ortega with the chief of staff of the army Gen. Joaquin de la Cuadra, who because of his social origins would be 'equal' or for the purpose of an accommodation with the elites.

28. Augusto Varas presented an advance draft of a research project on public opinion regarding the armed forces in the metropolitan area of Santiago, Chile, towards the end of 1991. In it he indicates that the military should not be the arbiters of national politics. They also have a weak commitment to democracy. See Varas, 'Civilians, the Military and Defense in a Restored Democracy: Public Opinion and the Armed Forces, the Chilean Case', Paper, ISA-RC01, Valparaiso, 1992.

29. We do not agree with the idea of 'professionalisation' which excludes political involvement. We cannot doubt the high level of professionalisation of the armed forces of the disappeared socialist bloc, during the 1960s and 1970s, despite the ideological political control they were subjected to. However, we must concede that a high level of involvement in daily political decisions deprives the military command of effective operational control of its forces.

30. The expression 'new international order', does not seem a felicitous one. Especially after the episodes of the rebirth of nationalsim and xenophobia in the various countries of Europe. New Order was the term used by Hitler to identify his regime

and its conquests and in general was the term used by Nazis, Fascists, Phalangists and other rightist groups in the 1930s and 1940s. Despite all of this we employ the term because of its common use in the current debate about the nature of the international system at the beginning of the 1990s.

31. The exceptions, Argentina, Brazil, and Chile, do not entirely negate our analysis, despite the fact that they have made important progress in this direction. The problem is that they could not consolidate them and, in good measure, in some of them the retrogression is obvious. The military industries did not become well established. Neither did the civilian sectors that produce military equipment progress much beyond the production of light equipment. Efforts to go beyond this have not overcome foreign pressures. In 'poor' countries, which are not leaders on a global scale, the ambition of having an economic sector linked to mililitary requirements is practically an illusion.

32. In studying the Bolivian case Raul Barrios Moron identifies the resurgence of nationalism as a result of this concern. See his 'El nacionalismo militar boliviano: elementos para la reformulacion estrategica', *Nueva Sociedad*, No.81, Caracas, 1986, pp.36–5, and 'Militares y democracia en Bolivia: entre la reforma o la desestabilizacion', Paper, ISA-RCO1, Valparaiso, 1992.

33. With regard to the traditional values of the military see Alfred Vagts, *Militarism, Civilian and Military* (NY: Meridian Books, 1959).

34. (London: Williams & Norgate, 1876–96), 3 vols.

35. For an intelligent analysis of the changes underway in the militaries of the first world see Charles Moskos and Frank Wood, *The Military: More Than Just a Job* (Elmsford Park, NY: Pergamon, 1987); and Bernard Boene (ed.), *La especificite militaire* (Paris: Armand Colin, 1990).

36. Brazil and Argentina received strong messages. Brazil had a nuclear development programme which now appears to have been stopped. The Argentine programme to develop medium-range missile called the Condor seems to have been abandoned or stopped. Argentina in 1991 signed the Missile Technology Control regime created in 1987 by the advanced countries. Along with Brazil they will adhere to the Tlatelolco Treaty to impede the development of nuclear weapons in Latin America. They further agreed to become members of the Australia Group which seeks the non-production of chemical weapons.

37. Along with the personnel of the 'Argentina' battalion deployed in Croatia, as well as the 'Uruguay' in Cambodia until 1993 and Mozambique at present, the US $933 in monthly compensation which the UN must pay is an amount which is very superior to what they receive for their work back home, especially in the lower levels of the forces. In Uruguay volunteers for the 840-man contingent to Cambodia were way over 3,000.

38. See the speech given by Pinochet on 21 Aug. 1992, in which he expresses the need to plan the modernisation of the Army in the new global context. Pinochet stated:

> The dangers which the hegemony of one superpower could generate . . . those who tend to forget the basic values of each nation . . . for which it is opportune to remember the validity of the old adage 'Roma locuta, causa finita' (when Rome speaks the cause is lost), a situation which, should it present itself, would not mean anything else than having gone backwards in two thousand years . . . Now, more than ever, we need clarity and stability in order to to prevent being absorbed by emerging powers and to face, with security and independence, the conjunction of stability and change.

(See the Chilean press on that day and the following).

39. See Charles Moskos, 'Armed Forces and Society after the Cold War', Paper, Wilson Center, Washington, DC, 1991.

40. Guatemala recognises the existence of Belize, Venezuela recognises Guyana and does not dispute the Esequibo. Venezuela and Colombia continue to find forms of agreement over the dispute regarding the Gulf of Maracaibo. El Salvador, Nicaragua,

and Honduras accepted the verdict of the Hague over their disputed areas. Argentina and Chile are putting an end to their boundary dispute by demarcating the Patagonian zone of ice fields. Peru has offered Bolivia an outlet at the port of Ilo, while Chile and Peru are making the final technical adjustments to Peruvian port rights in Arica. Bolivia's dispute with Chile affects the foreign relations of both. While Ecuador and Peru have lately undertaken confidence-bulilding measures, there remain problems because Ecuador has renounced the Rio de Janeiro Protocol of 1942 and disputes the demarcation of the border over the Cordillera of the Condor. Additionally, the Fujimori government has suggested schemes for the bilateral development of the frontier areas and navigational rights for the Ecuadorans in the Amazon Basin.

41. Guatemala and Peru have the most serious problems. On a minor scale they exist in Bolivia and Ecuador. For the moment they are containable within the national borders, but they could easily go beyond.

42. Shining Path, despite the arrest of its leader Abimael Guzman in Sept. 1992, continues to be an important threat to Peru. This is so in spite of the fact that the imposition of the 'militarist' line over the 'political' one that Guzman favoured could accelerate the decomposition of the movement.

43. The disturbances which marked the end of the Alfonsin government were contained by the police forces, but it would have been very difficult for the military to participate, because of the lack of troops, if the disturbances had become worse. Venezuela in 1989 needed to use the military in a brutal manner, because of the unexpected character of the disturbances. To prevent this situation the government of Sixto Duran in Ecuador mobilised the armed forces pre-emptively in Sept. 1992. Most of the troops did not show much enthusiasm for this task, which they also did not anticipate.

44. We do not use the term narcoterrorism because it combines different concepts, such as terrorism with narcotrafficking, which are not on the same level. Their conjunction means nothing more than the use of a form of violence to facilitate an activity. Neither can it be considered a synonym for subversion, which means a political activity designed to destabilise the social, economic, and political system with terrorism, which is only a symptom, and which can be employed by subversives or by other groups.

45. As in socialist societies where they pretended to work and in exchange they pretended to receive pay, for the 'struggle against drugs' they make us believe that there is eradication and in exchange the conscience of the better part of the citizenry of the United States can be at ease. Yet in many cases the result is not the one expected. Many favour general legalisation, among them respected economists such as Milton Friedman. The failure of the Temperance League and the 'dry' law taught lessons. On the other hand one forgets that the success achieved in reducing smoking was through education and not through a costly and violent campaign.

46. The polemic about the decline of the United States has had a following in the senior military colleges of the region. The book by Paul Kennedy, *The Rise and Fall of the Great Powers: Economic Change and Military Conflict From 1500 to 2000* (NY: Random House, 1987), has been widely distributed and translated into Spanish and Potuguese. The work of Joseph Nye, *Bound to Lead: The Changing Nature of American Power* (NY: Basic Books, 1990), which is more optimistic, has had less impact.

47. In Sept. 1993 only Argentina, Colombia, Chile, and Uruguay had civilian ministers of defence. In the other countries there are military ministers, in almost all cases retired military, or three ministries (Army, Navy, Air Force) exist, as occurs in Brazil. The power of the ministers is practically zero in Chile and Uruguay, where they are mere administrators or intermediaries with little control over the armed forces.

The Military, the Drug War and Democracy in Latin America: What Would Clausewitz Tell Us?

KENNETH E. SHARPE

Democracy and the Drug War

There is an obvious but superficial sense in which the drug trade threatens democracy in Latin American countries: powerful drug cartels become illegal and often uncontrollable corporations which can avoid taxes, corrupt government officials, raise private armies, and use force and terror to intimidate publicly elected officials, join with right wing landlords to kill local leaders of citizens' organisations, and in some cases make alliances with military officers who bring authoritarian, pro-drug regimes to places like Panama (General Manuel Antonio Noriega) or Bolivia (General Luis Garcia Meza).

Yet such conclusions are only partial, and thus superficial. For one thing, the major allies of the United States in the drug war are sometimes anti-democratic, and their very participation in the war creates incentives which further threatens democracy. Some US military allies, for example, have abysmal human rights records. The State Department's 1990 *Country* Report condemns the Peruvian military for 'widespread and egregious human rights violations'. The report asserts that 'the constitutional rights of persons detained by the military are routinely ignored' and 'suspected subversives held by the Government are routinely tortured at military detention centers . . . credible reports of rape by elements of the security forces in the emergency zone were so numerous that such abuse can be considered a common practice, condoned – or at least ignored – by the military leadership.'[1] In March 1991 Congressional testimony, Bernard Aronson, Assistant Secretary of State for Inter-American Affairs described abuses by the Peruvian security forces as 'long standing and systematic'. This same Peruvian military had no compunctions about its April 1992 support of President Alberto Fujimori's unilateral decision to suspend Peru's constitution and disband congress.

Human rights abuses are an equally serious concern in Colombia. The US House Committee on Government Operations concluded in a

November 1990 report: 'The committee is deeply concerned that US military aid may exacerbate human rights abuses in Colombia, in the context of the military's counterinsurgency campaign and extensive links between members of the Colombian military and drug-financed paramilitary death squads.'[2] The State Department's 1989 Human Rights Report on Colombia stated that 'Rural-based local military commanders have sometimes assisted right-wing groups, seeing them as allies against the guerrillas. Some of these same groups have been linked to narco-traffickers. In the past years little was done to stop such actions. Military officers have attempted to repeatedly obstruct prosecution of military personnel who committed human rights abuses.'[3] Thousands of Colombians have died during the past decade as a result of the 'dirty war' carried out by military-linked death squads against leftist politicians, union leaders, human rights workers, and other opponents of the status quo.

In Bolivia, US military aid for the drug war is opposed across much of the political spectrum because there is fear that strengthening the military can only weaken the country's nascent democratic institutions. Bolivian sociologist Raul Barrios argues 'increasing the military's potential in Bolivia is a serious matter. By augmenting its autonomy, the United States may very well be breaking down the military's subordination to civilian powers.'[4] Bolivian political scientist Eduardo Gamarra testified before US Congress in 1990 that 'Bolivia's efforts to consolidate democracy and promote economic growth, however, may well be torn apart by the very US strategies offered to support them.'[5] Such concerns cannot be taken lightly: Bolivia has experienced 182 military coups in its 168 years of independence.

There is a further complication in the superficial picture first presented: the possibility for democracy in Latin America rests in part on the possibility of re-activating long term growth in the region, and distributing the rewards of that growth broadly enough so that elected officials maintain their legitimacy. One of the major threats to democracy in Latin America – the food riots and attempted coup in Venezuela, one of the most stable of all Latin American democracies is a harbinger here – is that the structural adjustment programmes are most hurting the poor and middle class in the new and often fragile democracies in the region. Democracy gives these people some power to make demands on the government to get growth growing or to ease austerity and relieve the conditions of poverty and decline which worsened in the lost decade of the 1980s. If these new democracies do not come through, they could lose their legitimacy and be subject to military coups; yet if governments try to meet the demands of the populace by rejecting United States,

World Bank, and International Monetary Fund (IMF) austerity guidelines they also risk economic de-stabilisation and coups. In several
Andean countries the only thing that 'floats' these economies in the
current period – and thus ironically removes pressure on democracy – is
the drug trade.

Bolivia provides a telling example. The economic crisis of the early
1980s – a decline in per capita income of 30 per cent between 1980 and
1984, inflation at 24,000 per cent in 1985, the 1985 collapse of its major
legal export, tin – led to economic shock treatment in 1985 – a drastic
stabilisation program based on IMF guidelines. When Jaime Paz
Zamora became president in late 1989 he continued the stabilisation
plan. By 1990 inflation was brought down to 18 per cent; there was an
annual growth of 2.5 per cent in Gross Domestic Product (GDP);
foreign debt was reduced by 12 per cent; and exports have risen
although Bolivia still pays 25 per cent of its total export earnings to
service its debt.

Yet rarely mentioned in Bolivia's economic 'success' story is one not-
so-secret ingredient: coca. The coca economy generates as much foreign
exchange as all other Bolivian exports combined, and provides a critical
cushion for many of those left unemployed as a result of the government's austerity program. Since 1985, for example, about 45,000 state
jobs in mining and public administration were eliminated; factory
shutdowns resulting from liberalised import policies led to another
35,000 layoffs. But the coca trade now employs about 20 per cent of the
work force: at least 300,000 Bolivians have jobs directly tied to it.

The $600 million generated every year from coca sales have been
critical for the economic stabilisation programme and the Bolivian
government implemented several measures in the late 1980s to facilitate
the absorption of drug profits into the banking system, such as a tax
amnesty on repatriated capital, relaxed disclosure requirements for the
Central Bank, and prohibitions against official investigations into the
origin of wealth brought into Bolivia. Cocaine profits in Caribbean
banks could come home safely.

The government also instituted a daily foreign exchange auction, the
bolsin, which allowed the Central Bank to soak up coca dollars normally
absorbed by the parallel foreign-exchange market; in effect this tacitly
legalise the circulation of drug money. These measures helped boost
Bolivia's foreign-exchange reserves. Short term deposits in dollars and
dollar-indexed accounts grew from less than $28 million in September
1985 to an estimated $279 million in March 1987. This in turn helped
stabilise the currency and curb hyperinflation.[6] Thus Bolivia's ability to
sustain its fragile democracy depended on moderating its economic

crisis and cushioning the effects of stabilisation – and the coca economy played a key role.

Given these complexities – that the drug trade is currently sustaining some economies that would otherwise be in a crisis which would threaten democracy, that the security forces enlisted in the drug war are likely to become more anti-democratic as a result of that war – how is the issue of the mission of the US military in the drug war to be addressed?

We could ask the question: how could the US military most effect-ively work with the Latin American militaries to fight the drug war in ways that would be less rather than more destructive to democracy? From this approach would follow some of the classic questions the military asked during and after Vietnam about limited war: how can local militaries be professionalised? How can they be inculcated in the value of human rights and a respect for the rule of law and democracy? How can corruption be tamed, discouraged, or controlled? How can North Americans work with them in ways that minimise nationalist, anti-Yankee resentment? How can joint operations be carried out that do not alienate the local population? Are there ways to convince the population to stop growing coca, stop supporting drug traffickers, and even turn in drug traffickers? Can the people's hearts and minds be won? Are there ways to provide economic alternatives to coca produc-tion – through crop substitution and credit programmes for example – that will provide a carrot along with the stick of force, and should the US military be involved in such economic programmes, or perhaps a broader civic action programme? Should there be special training for US military personnel which will introduce them to elements of police training since drug conflicts involve civil-police relations as much if not more than civil-military relations?

I will return to some of these questions below but in the context of a different question which I think is prior and more central: is this a war that the US military ought to be fighting? If it is not, we should not be tinkering with how to fight it in ways that minimise the harm to democracy.

In the United States the question of whether the military ought to be fighting this war is a fundamental political question to be settled by the American people, through their elected representatives in Congress and the President. But a fundamental consideration in answering this question is what kind of instrument is the US military – and is the kind of force it is skilled at applying the appropriate instrument for dealing with the drug trade abroad in order to solve drug problems on America's streets? Here the lessons of Clausewitz as interpreted by current military theorists, like Harry G. Summers,[7] recent Secretaries of Defense, like Caspar W. Weinberger, and the former Chairman of the Joint Chiefs of Staff, Colin General L. Powell, provide some guidance.

On Strategy: When is Military Force Appropriate?

Military strategy, Summers points out referring to the Joint Chiefs of Staff Dictionary of Military and Associated Terms, is 'the art and science of employing the armed forces of a nation to secure the objectives of national policy by the application of force, or the threat of force.'[8] What emerges from Summers and other military strategists who have re-vitalised Clausewitz is a clear understanding of what it means to employ armed force to secure the objectives of national policy. First it means that there must be a clear mission: like in Panama (1989) or the 1991 Gulf War, but unlike Beirut in 1982–84 or Vietnam in the 1960s. What is to be avoided say these strategists, is unwise or ill-defined missions, and there is a special scepticism regarding the use of the military as a 'signal' to let the enemy know US intentions.

If American armed forces are not to be used as signalling devices, then what is their utility?

> Simply stated, they exist to kill people and destroy things in the name of the American people. Their utility lies almost entirely in their ability to accomplish those terrible deeds. And it is the threat of their doing so that makes than an effective instrument of American foreign policy. As the great military theorist Karl von Clausewitz pointed out, in war, everything depends on battle, for the outcome rests on the perception that if you did fight, you would win.[9]

'You must begin', said Colin Powell in September 1992, 'with a clear understanding of what political objective is being achieved.'[10] 'A clear military objective – not just a vague injunction to "stop the drug traffickers" – must be specified', as Caspar Weinberger put it.[11]

A related second principle is that 'decisive means and results are always to be preferred, even if they are not always possible.'[12] Military force is best used to achieve a decisive victory. As General Powell said, 'As soon as they tell me it's limited, it means they do not care whether you achieve a result or not. As soon as they tell me "surgical", I head for the bunker.'[13] The argument here is that force levels must be high enough to achieve victory. Yet there is a firm understanding among such strategists that force is not always the best way to secure the objectives of national policy, so a third principle is that military force is not always the appropriate response to a problem or a threat. 'Military force', said Powell 'is not always the right answer. If force is used imprecisely or out of frustration rather than clear analysis, the situation can be made worse.'[14]

Finally, and very importantly for these strategists, in a democracy the mission assigned to the military – the national objective – must have the support of the American people. 'Public Support is an essential precondition for the conduct of military operations',[15] writes Summers. In Weinberger's words: 'before the US commits combat forces aboard, there must be some reasonable assurance we will have the support of the American people and their elected representatives in Congress.'[16]

Such principles – and this is only a partial list – provide some guidance in answering the question whether the military should have a major mission in the war on drugs.

The War on Drugs in Latin America

Perhaps the first thing that should be said about the US military in the war on drugs is a brief comment about capability. There is evidence that elements of the US military are quite capable at carrying out specific tasks: they can, for example, interdict shipments on the high seas and more funds and equipment would allow them to interdict more tons; they can spot coca from the air; track planes in the skies; and, as Operation 'Blast Furnace' demonstrated in Bolivia, effectively work with local forces to destroy labs.

Yet the issue here is not the ability to accomplish particular tasks. The issue is rather one of the use of force to accomplish political objectives. And the principles outlined above should give us cause for concern.

The Military and the US Drug Control Strategy: Is the Mission Clear?

The political objective of military force – and the clarity of the mission – must be understood in the context of the overall US drug control strategy.

United States counter-narcotics strategies in the Andean region are grounded in a theory about the drug problem here at home. Most policy-makers agree that the problem of drug use and abuse has a demand side – Americans are able and eager to buy drugs; and a supply side – drugs are cheaply and readily available. The President's National Drug Control Strategy combines strategies to curb demand through treatment and prevention with measures to reduce supply through enforcement and interdiction. The overwhelming focus of the national drug strategy, however, is on the supply side: 70 per cent of 1991 federal anti-drug dollars are invested in supply reduction programmes; only 30 per cent target demand. The assumption is that severely restricting supply will lower Americans' demand for drugs by making them scarcer and more expensive – thus reducing domestic consumption.

Supply-side tactics include law enforcement programmes to disrupt distribution at home and interdiction efforts on borders. Abroad, the US drug control effort aims at seizing drug shipments by land, sea, and air, at disabling trafficking networks, and at destroying the drug supply at the source of production before it is transported through trafficking networks to US city streets.

In the current war on cocaine and its cheap derivative 'crack', the targets are the Andean cocaine-producing countries of Peru, Bolivia and Colombia. In the late 1980s drug strategists converged on the need for a more aggressive strategy 'at the source'. 'The logic is simple', President George Bush said. 'The cheapest and safest way to eradicate narcotics is to destroy them at their source . . . We need to wipe out crops wherever they are grown and take out labs wherever they exist.' Former US ambassador to Bolivia Edwin Corr professed, 'The closer you get to where it comes from, the more bang you get for your buck.'

The US drug war in the Andes is built around the twin tactics of law enforcement and economic assistance. The *enforcement* component seeks to cut supply by eradicating peasant coca crops, destroying processing laboratories, blocking the transport of processing chemicals, and interdicting coca, cocaine and chemical shipments. Traffickers are to be arrested and prosecuted, their assets seized and operations dismantled.

Past US drug control efforts emphasised the use of Andean civilian law enforcement agencies – the police, prosecutors, courts, and prisons; Washington sought to strengthen these agencies with aid, technical assistance, and equipment. Meagre results led to a search for ways to increase enforcement capabilities. An early step was to 'militarise' the police. Beginning in 1983 the US helped establish special counter-narcotics police units in Bolivia and Peru. The units were in fact paramilitary squads within the police, trained by US Special Forces personnel. When this proved insufficient, Federal narcotics officials increasingly looked to Andean militaries – backed by US equipment and training – to do the job.

The enforcement strategy has been coupled with an *economic assistance* component. A 1990 report by the Office of National Drug Control Policy emphasises that 'economic strategies and resources are required to provide the general conditions for a healthy and viable legal economy throughout the region as well as provide viable alternatives for those currently engaged in illicit drug cultivation.' In practice this has meant balance of payments support and crop substitution programmes to encourage peasants to abandon coca for alternative crops.

It was the failure of this strategy to stem drug production and trafficking in the 1980s that led the Bush administration to escalate. Unveiled in September 1989, the President's Andean Initiative was a five-year, $2.2 billion programme that provided unprecedented levels of US aid for Colombia, Peru and Bolivia to escalate enforcement and economic assistance. The Andean strategy stated four near-term goals:

(1) To strengthen the political commitment and institutional capability of the Governments of Colombia, Peru, and Bolivia to disrupt, and ultimately dismantle, trafficking organizations;

(2) To increase the effectiveness of law enforcement and security activities of the three countries against the cocaine trade. This involves providing law enforcement and military assistance to enable them to fight the traffickers in remote and inaccessible areas in which drug production activities often take place;

(3) To inflict significant damage on the trafficking organizations that predominate within the three countries . . .; and

(4) To strengthen and diversify the legitimate economies of the Andean nations to enable them to overcome the destabilizing effects of eliminating cocaine, a major source of income.[17]

The major shift in the Andean enforcement strategy was the dramatic but quite predictable extension of militarisation: Washington signed separate military assistance agreements with Peru, Bolivia, and Colombia, assigning leading roles for their respective military forces in the war on drugs, and committing extensive US training and equipment. Local militaries received the bulk of US law enforcement assistance. The militarisation of the drug war also required a significantly expanded training role for the US Department of Defense and American advisers were being sent to the region. In Peru, where the Bush administration has concluded that the Shining Path guerrillas were impeding drug enforcement, the US considered again involving itself in counter-insurgency.[18]

Once the Andean countries adopted this militarised enforcement strategy, economic assistance followed. The $2.2 billion programmed for the region was targeted at balance of payments support rather than specific alternative development programs. The governments of Peru and Bolivia strongly resisted Washington's initial efforts to draw their militaries into the drug control campaign, yet their desperate need for US economic and support gave them little choice but to sign the accords.

Given this drug control strategy, grave difficulties emerge for those anxious to define a clear political objective that will define a clear mission for the US military. The political objective of our drug control strategy ought to be the reduction of drug addiction and abuse at home, and the reduction of drug-related violence. But the only possible role for the military in accomplishing this objective is the reduction of the amount of narcotics entering the United States. But what does 'reduction' mean? A 'vague injunction to "stop the drug traffickers" ' is not a clear military objective, as Caspar Weinberger pointed out.[19] Nor does any serious analyst think that 'sealing the borders' is a clear, let alone feasible, objective. It is unclear – indeed highly contested as we will see below – what level of 'reduced overseas supply' would have a significant impact on raising the cost of drugs at home; and it is even unclear the extent to which raising cost would lower drug abuse, drug addiction, or drug-related violence.

The first three near term goals of the Andean strategy (the goals which focus on military and law enforcement efforts) themselves provide little clarity. Strengthening 'political commitment and institutional capability' sounds as vague and problematic as the Vietnam era goal of 'nation building'. 'Increasing the effectiveness of law enforcement and security activities' is something US military advisers could do but leaves unclear the framework for judging effectiveness: effective toward what political or military end? 'Inflicting significant damage on trafficking organizations' assumes without argument that significant damage (whatever that is) would have a notable long-term effect on supply and price in the US and thus on abuse, addiction, and drug-related violence.

The vagueness about political objectives creates a temptation to reduce mission to measurement – to set goals in terms of the tons of cocaine seized, the number of labs destroyed, the acres of crops eradicated. Yet these drug war equivalents of 'body counts' are meaningless without clarity about objectives: without first knowing what the military objective is and how such indicators are related to that objective there is no way to interpret the numbers; and there is the further problem that these numbers only make sense in terms of the total number of labs, crop acreage and shipments; the real amounts that are arriving on US shores; and the relation of these supplies to demand, abuse, addiction and violence. It is also unclear whether reduction means 'reduction in Peru, Bolivia, and Columbia' or also means reduction in Mexico, Central America and the Caribbean; or whether reduction also includes the new countries in Latin America to which the trade is spreading (e.g., Brazil, Argentina, Ecuador) as a result of the drug war in the Andes; or whether reduction should be thought of on a worldwide scale to also include narcotics from Burma, Thailand, Afghanistan, Eastern Europe, and even Kazakhstan and Kyrgyzstan in Central Asia;[20] or whether the objective should also be the reduction of the drug production within the US (a major producer of marijuana and synthetic narcotics).

The lack of a clear mission creates grave dangers for the application of military force to the drug war because the central political purpose of sending in the military can become a kind of signalling. One kind of signalling is to the drug traffickers and drug producing peasants: the US is serious about getting you to stop producing and trafficking; here is a taste of what is in store if you do not if. Yet if the traffic and production does not abate – and below I will argue that significant abatement is unlikely – then the military is in exactly the position many strategists want to avoid: continued escalation to send continued signals that are ineffective.

A second kind of signalling is a symbolic signalling to the US public by elected officials. 'Elect me because I'm tough on drugs and I can prove my toughness by escalating the use of force in Latin America: I'm for sending in the US military to get the job done.' Using the military to send electoral signals to the US public is not exactly the kind of national policy objective that Clausewitz and his current students have in mind.

Decisive Means and Results: Can the US Military Secure National Objectives?

The lack of clarity about objectives and mission makes it difficult to evaluate the drug war in terms of other principles – is this a kind of war in which the means and results can be decisive, and is military force the best way to secure these objectives? Yet evidence from the Latin drug war front – indeed evidence from decades of drug war efforts – should raise serious doubts.

There is evidence that the US drug control strategy of the 1980s, and the newer Andean initiative, have by and large failed to cut supplies, raise domestic prices, and reduce abuse, addiction, and drug-related violence in significant amounts – and this despite the fact that there have been very successful raids, seizures, and arrests of major drug traffickers. The results of the drug war before the Andean strategy indicated that enforcement and economic assistance strategies were failing to significantly reduce supply at the source. The Drug Enforcement Agency (DEA) estimate that cocaine production in South

America skyrocketed from about 361 metric tons in 1988 to 900 metric tons in 1990. Coca cultivation approached 200,000 tons of coca leaf a year, enough to satisfy four times the estimated US cocaine market.[21]

By the end of the 1980s all three Andean countries witnessed a substantial net *increase* in coca cultivation, despite US-sponsored crop and seedbed eradication campaigns: eradication levels consistently failed even to keep peace with new growth.[22] Interdiction efforts yielded equally dismal results, particularly in Peru and Bolivia. In 1989, for example, less than one per cent of Peruvian coca paste and base was seized; in Bolivia, seizures by US and Bolivian forces totalled a mere one-half of one per cent.

Enforcement efforts in Colombia have shown periodic signs of success – but even these have been short-lived. In the months following the Colombian government's renowned autumn 1989 crackdown, cocaine-processing and trafficking activities dropped by over 70 per cent. US officials in Bogotá confirmed, however, that production quickly recovered, reaching 80 per cent of the previous level within months.

In March 1989 the Office of the Inspector General at the State Department concluded that despite 'significant achievements' in seizures, labs destroyed, and arrests, 'the INM (the Bureau of International Narcotics Matters) agrees that the programs have had little impact on the availability of illicit narcotics in the United States.'

Preliminary evidence indicates that the results of the Andean strategy will not be much different: increased success in terms of crops eradicated, labs destroyed, and traffickers arrested but little or no reduction in overall levels of supply. Washington claimed progress, but official reports of failure to achieve real supply reductions continued to mount. The State Department's March 1991 report acknowledged that the Department underestimated the potential dry leaf coca harvest in Peru and Bolivia over the last five years by about one-third; anticipated 'a larger increase in leaf production [in Peru's Upper Huallaga Valley] in 1991'; and noted that even with increased law enforcement efforts in Bolivia, 'trafficking organizations have kept pace by diversifying their marketing of refined cocaine . . .' Officials acknowledged that successes up to late 1991 in curbing the operations of the Medellín cartel in Colombia, meanwhile, have led only to an increased market share for the Cali cartel, Medellín's main competitor: according to DEA chief Robert Bonner, the Cali cartel has boosted its market share to 75 per cent from 30 per cent during the first ten months of the government crackdown on Medellín.[23]

A September 1991 General Accounting Office (GAO) report concluded that the billions of dollars the nation had spent on anti-smuggling efforts had failed to reduce the flow of cocaine into the US. The GAO noted that efforts to raise drug traffickers' operating costs by creating obstacles is unlikely to succeed since cocaine is so cheap and plentiful in South America and it is doubtful that costs can be increased 'to an extent that would affect trafficking operations'. Federal officials report that 70 to 90 per cent of the cocaine destined for the America's streets gets past them. The GAO concluded that 'the estimated flow of cocaine into the United States did not decrease in 1989 and 1990.'[24]

Will increased US military involvement turn this situation around? Political expediency may encourage some to respond to failure with escalation – one can always argue that not enough resources have been put in, that there is light at the end of the tunnel, or that you have just begun to fight – but a hard look at the realities in the region gives reason for pause. Two of the key conditions for the drug war strategy to succeed are these: First, the Andean governments, police, and militaries must have the will and capability to carry out US narcotics control strategies. Second, the peasant producers must have the will and capability to stop growing and processing coca. Absent these local conditions, success depends on the will and ability of the United States to create the requisite conditions.

Interestingly, Washington officials recognise that the will and capability to fight the drug war do not now exist in the Andean countries, and the 1990 report of the Office of National Drug Control Policy underlines that 'strengthening political will and institutional capability . . . is a requisite for all further [counternarcotics] actions in the Andean region.' There is something disturbingly similar here to past justifications for limited wars and low intensity conflicts. Not decisive means for decisive results; not an argument that sufficient force will achieve national objectives; but rather an open-ended faith that if local allies can be given the ability and will to fight the war ('nation building') and if the populace can be wooed to the anti-drugs side (win their 'hearts and minds') then local forces will be able to succeed (whatever that means).

Analysis of the on-the-ground realities through much of the region give little reason to believe that the US military could create the requisite will or capability among local governments, militaries, or peasants.

Will and Capability: The Andean Governments, Police, and Militaries

The evidence that Andean governments, police, and militaries lack the requisite *capability* to fight the drug war has been documented widely by counter-narcotics officials, and provides the central rationale for the escalation outlined in the Andean strategy. Andean militaries and police are presently no match for narco-trafficking organisations operating transnationally and backed by private armies, advanced weaponry, and highly sophisticated intelligence systems. Andean security forces are further hamstrung by operational inefficiency and ineffectiveness.

A November 1989 raid on the eastern Bolivian town of San Ramon, touted by the US Embassy as 'the largest counter-narcotics enforcement operation in recent times' is a case in point. The raid was compromised by a tip-off; the targeted Colombian and Bolivian traffickers fled the site over 12 hours before the operation. Less than five kilos of cocaine HCl were seized; the 20 Bolivians detained during the raid were released for lack of evidence, and the entire operation was estimated to have cost more than $100,000 . . .[25]

Countless such examples of operational inefficiencies and mismanagement led a DEA internal review to conclude by underlining the need for 'institution-building.'

> All members of the study team agree that 'institution-building', or helping host country law enforcement agencies develop to the point of operational self-sufficiency, has been an objective of the United States foreign policy for years. . . . Despite significant achievements, institution-building in the [Andean drug-producing] countries is incomplete. No . . . country is currently able to routinely conduct operations against coca processors without a US presence.[26]

What leverage does the US have to create this institutional capability? In certain areas, Washington can and will make a difference. It can put resources into training judiciaries, establishing new courts for drug proceedings, providing credit and technical assistance for crop substitution. It can improve the *efficiency* of enforcement agencies by providing police and military training (intelligence and operations), equipment (radar, helicopters), and US advisers. The size and operational capacity of the counter-narcotics units will grow and improved operational efficiency should lead to measurable, short-term successes: an increase in number of crops eradicated, coca paste seized, labs destroyed and traffickers arrested.

But such *efficiency* does not necessarily translate into the *effectiveness* that is the real mark of the capability of institutions to meet stated objectives – in this case, cocaine supply reduction. This gap between efficiency and effectiveness is systematically hidden by the very measures of 'success' favoured by policy advocates. There is a tendency to emphasise the number of crops eradicated and not the amount of new coca planted; the number of labs destroyed and not the number rebuilt or the total processing capability; the number of seizures and not the totals being shipped; the number of arrests and not the continued effectiveness of the trafficking networks. With such measures, there is no failure, only milestones toward success – because means have become ends.

These misleading measures obscure a deeper problem: no degree of technical capability among Andean drug enforcement agencies can achieve US objectives unless government and military officials are committed to making our war their war. And their *will* to fight seems notably absent.

The reasons for the lack of Andean commitment to the US drug war are not hard to identify. The current economic and political realities of the drug trade make it rational for local actors – Andean political leaders, military and law enforcement officials, and millions of peasants, producers and others involved in the trade – to follow strategies that diverge significantly from US counter-narcotics objectives. The limits on Washington's ability to create the will to fight may be far greater than even the most pragmatic of American drug strategists have calculated.

1. National Interests: Why the Drug War is not a Priority. US officials acknowledge the lack of political will among Andean governments. Kirk Kotula, INM's Bolivia programme officer, noted in a January 1990 memo that the Bolivian government's performance 'in almost every area indicates total lack of commitment to the anti-drug war.'[27] The DEA has reached similar conclusions about Peru.[28]

The primary concerns of Peruvian President Alberto Fujimori and Bolivian President Jaime Paz Zamora are to ensure economic and political stability in long impoverished nations that are now also suffering from high unemployment, hyper-inflation, and falling wages. Immediate economic and political interests dictate against a crackdown on coca, both nations' most significant and dependable source of dollars and jobs. The Peruvian coca economy brings in approximately $1 billion annually, or 30 per cent of the total value of exports, and employs some 15 per cent of the national work force. The Bolivian situation is more severe as we saw earlier: Bolivia's $600 million in annual coca revenues is equivalent to the value of all other exports combined and the coca industry employs 300,000 Bolivians, or one fifth of the adult work force.

A serious effort to destroy the coca economy would have a devastating economic and political impact – one which Andean leaders are in no position to absorb. The livelihoods of hundreds of thousands of citizens would be threatened, triggering massive social unrest. President Jaime Paz Zamora contrasted the effect of eliminating the Bolivian coca industry to laying off 50 million Americans by closing down a single industry.

The political impact of the drug war is further complicated in Peru by the Shining Path insurgency, identified by Peruvian leaders as their second greatest concern.[29] Peru's Upper Huallaga Valley is effectively controlled by Shining Path; the insurgents portray themselves as protectors of the peasant growers, often serving as intermediaries on their behalf with the traffickers. An aggressive narcotics control effort would increase the immediate threat posed by the guerrillas, by driving peasants into their ranks. Peruvian politicians, according to a 1989 DEA internal review,

> have made the statement that Peru can live with the narcotics problem for the next fifty years, but may not survive the next two years if the economic and insurgent problems are not dealt with now. . . . The will to deal with the drug issue, when faced with problems that threaten the immediate survival of the country, remains the most difficult issue.[30]

The question of political will is more complex but equally at issue in Colombia: the government's priority is not ending drug trafficking *per se*, but ending the violence associated with the drug trade. The violence generated by Colombian traffickers has taken a heavy toll in lives and internal peace and stability. In the 'total war' declared by the Medellín drug cartel in 1989, over 400 police officers, 100 judges and judicial assistants, and 11 journalists were killed in one year.[31] Although the government's war on drugs was held up as the shining model of US counter-narcotics strategies in action, the Gaviria government has drawn clear distinction between *narcoterrorism* and *narcotrafficking*. The government's interest was, and still is, the reduction of drug-related violence, generated primarily by the notorious Medellín cartel; the crackdown on the Medellín group has been formidable. Yet Colombian officials show little commitment to stopping the drug-trafficking activities of a broad range of other drug networks, including the major competitor to Medellín, the Cali cartel. As long as other drug trafficking organisations do not use paramilitary violence to threaten the government, it is unlikely that they will be aggressively targeted.

The challenge of creating political will is not lost on US narcotics officials. 'Political will, pragmatically speaking, I would define as getting governments to do something they do not want to do', stated INM narcotics specialist Daniel Chaij.[32] He and others, however, act as if the right mix of carrots and sticks can make Andean governments act in accordance with US strategy. They fail to understand the systemic character of the problem: the divergent interests of the Andean governments are deeply rooted in obdurate structures and are unlikely to bend with pressure or persuasion. It is highly unlikely that any US drug strategy designed to reduce the supply of cocaine in the source countries can reconcile the problem of conflicting national priorities. The economies of Peru and Bolivia are deeply dependent on coca for revenues and employment. Moreover, the social unrest generated by a crackdown on the drug trade would alienate the government from the social base it needs to conduct its polices. In the case of Peru and potentially Bolivia, the drug control strategy drives peasants into the hands of guerrilla groups, fueling insurgencies that threaten the very existence of the government. For Andean leaders, suppression of the cocaine supply to the American market cannot replace an interest as fundamental as economic and political survival.

Certainly Andean governments share an interest in receiving American aid and support: offering millions of dollars in desperately needed aid in return for a commitment to fight the drug war, not surprisingly, has generated formal commitments and varying levels of cooperation from each of the Andean nations. Yet the absence of a genuine commitment to US anti-drug objectives suggests that only those components of the drug policy that serve existing local interests – such as economic assistance programs for peasants, and military aid for counter-insurgency – will be actively pursued.

2. *Competing Bureaucratic Interests.* Andean will to wage the drug war is further undermined by the competing interests of law enforcement and military institutions charged with carrying out the US counter-insurgency strategy. Military and police, for example, frequently refuse to cooperate and will even sabotage each other's operations. US field reports document the inter-agency conflicts as security forces vie for resources, prestige, and power in each of the three nations in a pattern not uncommon among Latin American security forces.

In some instances, notably Peru, these inter-agency conflicts are exacerbated by the contradictory missions of police and military forces. The Peruvian military is wholly absorbed in a countersurgency campaign against the Shining Path; the responsibilities of the police, on the other hand, include narcotics control missions conducted independently or with DEA assistance. The conflict is played out in the Upper Huallaga Valley. The military's interest is in driving a wedge between the insurgents and the coca-growing peasants whom the guerrillas claim to protect; military forces therefore are reluctant to alienate the growers and have generally permitted them to grow coca unimpeded. The police, on the other hand, seek to disrupt both growing and trafficking activities. The two missions are fundamentally at odds, and lead not only to a lack of cooperation, but also to disputes that have flared into armed confrontations. State Department officials acknowledge a 'repeated pattern of incidents' in which Peruvian military forces have thwarted DEA operations, including through armed confrontation. General Alberto Arciniega, formerly regional commander in the valley, explained, 'There are 150,000 *campesino cocaleros* [peasant coca-growers] in the zone. Each of them is a potential *subversivo*. Eradicate his field and the next day he'll be one.' 'Most of my troops come from this area', he notes. 'In effect, the police were wiping our the livelihood of their families, while I was asking them to fight Shining Path, which was sworn to protect the growers. Shining Path looked like heroes.'[33]

The dramatic increase in military involvement in the drug war under the Andean Initiative exacerbates police-military conflicts over drug war objectives. Administration attempts to link the two missions did get counter-insurgency aid from a Congress concerned about drugs, but it papered over the fundamental contradiction between fight the drug war and fighting Shining Path. The military's primary mission will still be counter-insurgency – although they will gladly pay lip service to the drug war to gain US military aid. According to a DEA assessment, 'Even if there was clear direction from the [Fujimori administration], inter-agency rivalries continue, while legal and jurisdictional problems with the Peruvian military persist.'[34]

Tensions exist between narcotics control and counter-insurgency campaigns in Colombia as well, where the clear priority of the military is also to battle insurgents, not drugs. In fact, Colombian military officials told US congressional staff that $38.5 million of the $40.3 million in counter-narcotics assistance allocated for 1990 would provide most of the logistical support for a major counter-insurgency operation in an area not known for drug trafficking.[35]

Can a well-crafted US policy solve the problem of institutional rivalry and conflicting missions that undermine the will of the Andean countries to fight America's drug war? There may be some specific actions Washington can take that would have some salutary effects on the margins. But given the inability of the Federal government to achieve adequate cooperation and coordination among its various agencies engaged in the drug war in Washington, the limits of US leverage in the more intractable Andean context are obvious. Reports of DEA special agents in Peru are particularly telling:

> without the DEA presence, the Peruvians would not move against the traffickers. If given an airlift capability, the Peruvians would be

more likely to move against the insurgents than the traffickers. Without US presence, human rights violations, including the slaughter of insurgents or traffickers, is likely.[36]

This conclusion suggests that while Washington may succeed in winning apparent compliance with its objectives and methods, once US agents turn their backs, the security forces will revert to their own mission and methods. There is no reason to believe that US policy will be any more successful in the future in creating the will to fight the drug war.

3. Institutional Corruption. Perhaps the most insidious and un-controllable factor undermining the local commitment to fight the drug war is the drug-related corruption that is rampant among the militaries and law enforcement agencies of all three nations. 'Corruption is a major factor within the police, the military and the judiciary' in Peru, according to DEA officials[37] and in Bolivia, the State Department reported in March 1991 that 'Widespread corruption, compounded by [government] weakness in policy implementation, further combine to hamper [the Government of Bolivia's] counter-narcotics effectiveness.' Endemic corruption in fact creates individual and institutional interests in furthering the drug trade.

Forms of corruption are wide-ranging. Agents 'tip off' narcotics traffickers before anti-drug operations. They accept payoffs to allow arrested traffickers to escape, or to allow drugs and processing chemicals to be transported through checkpoints. Roadblocks in Bolivia's Chapare region have become profitable ventures for some police personnel: the problem is so widespread that DEA and Bolivian Anti-Narcotics Police agents routinely run through checkpoints on their way to a raid in order to prevent checkpoint personnel from calling ahead to inform traffickers of the impending operation. Corruption has flared inter-agency tensions into armed conflict between security forces. In two incidents in March 1990, Peruvian police anti-drug units flying over the Upper Huallaga valley in US-owned helicopters were fired upon by Peruvian military forces.[38] Similarly, two Bolivian police helicopters were crippled by gunfire in a night-time assault on the town of Santa Ana. The helicopters were hit by the Bolivian Navy detachment stationed in the town, according to US Embassy reports.[39]

Unless the corruption deeply embedded in the government, police and military can be addressed, the very agents on which Washington relies to carry out the strategy will effectively subvert the drug war in pursuit of personal and institutional interests in the drug trade. What leverage does the United States have in tempering this problem?

Distressingly little. The US can and on occasion has secured the removal of individual officials accused of corruption. In spring 1991, for example, US officials pressed successfully for the removal of Bolivia's Colonel Foustino Rico Toro as head of counter-narcotics operations, whom the US had accused of narcotics-related corruption. But these incremental responses to American pressure are temporising measures perceived by Andean leaders as necessary to secure continued assistance from Uncle Sam.

The drug-related corruption is systemic, not simply a problem of a few individuals or a particular group. The high profits of the drug trade make corruption rational for government officers and military officials whose salaries cannot compete with traffickers bribes. Moreover, an intensified anti-narcotics campaign heightens the risks involved in the drug trade, thereby increasing the need for traffickers to rely on bribes and pay-offs. The more aggressive the counter-narcotics campaign, the greater the corruption and the higher the institutional stakes in the drug trade – and in subverting the drug war. In the late 1970s the Colombian Army was directed to wage war on marijuana production, but the operations resulted in such corruption that it was soon withdrawn.[40] Because the US strategy is unable to reduce the profitability of the trade, corruption will increase at each of three levels.

The most common form of corruption involves individuals who accept money simply to look the other way or conveniently disappear during a drug transaction. The motivation is not complicated: In 1989 testimony, retired Special Forces Commander General Robert C. Kingston described a conversation with a US Border Patrol agent at a checkpoint in Peru:

> A colonel from Lima said, I have the opportunity while I'm here to make $70,000 by looking the other way at certain times. You have a family, they are protected in the United States, you have a proper pension plan. My family is not protected and I don't have the proper pension plan and I will never have the opportunity to make $70,000 as long as I live. I am going to make it.[41]

A senior officer in Peru earns about $240 a month. It should therefore be no surprise that officers bribe their superiors to get assigned to coca-producing zones seen as sources of easy money. Areas once considered as outposts to be avoided at all costs are now the most sought-after assignments.

Corruption becomes more insidious, however, when elements of an institution are complicit in the traffic itself, and the institution acts as a shield against individual accountability. In Bolivia, for example, US equipment has been used by complicit police personnel to ferry drugs or precursor chemicals to production sites. Seized coca products have been re-sold for a profit following a raid.[42]

In Peru, military and government authorities actually charge drug traffickers for the use of air strips – like the one in the Upper Huallaga town of Uchiza – where cocaine paste is flown out of Peru. The protection charge at Uchiza is said to be $25,000 per flight. Further, the army blocks Peruvian and US anti-drug squads from interfering.[43]

On a larger scale, bank records located after the capture and killing of Colombian trafficker Gonzalo Rodriguez Gacha revealed that he had provided multi-million dollar payoffs to *entire brigades* of the Colombian Army which has only 12 such units.[44] In one well-known 1983 case, a Colombian special forces company helped relocate an entire cocaine-processing operation that was threatened by guerrilla attacks. The operation took nearly a month and involved almost 50 army personnel, including six officers; each was paid between $500 and $2,500 by the traffickers. Asked why he did not act to seize the cocaine laboratory, the Chief of Staff of the 7th Brigade responded that 'it is not the mission' of the Army to fight drugs but rather to battle insurgents.'[45] In late 1989 the Colombian office of the Attorney General had 1,700 cases of corruption involving the armed forces under investigation.[46]

Corruption reaches its highest form when national leaders use the power of the state to further personal stakes in the drug trade. Panama's Manuel Noriega is the most notorious example of state-level drug corruption. Yet the Andean nations have had their own drug dictators. Andean expert Gustavo Gorriti testified before Congress that the 1980 to 1982 Garcia Meza regime in Bolivia was without a doubt the most important case in which political power – the control of a country – was used to further, protect and engage in narcotics trafficking.[47]

Drug policy officials in Washington often concede the absence of Andean will to fight the US drug war, but they are studiously silent on how to create it. Officials acknowledge that the task is a formidable one: 'The "moral" factors of corruption and national will' are more complex than the 'physical' factors of training and equipment, observes a DEA report, 'requiring progress in tangible and intangible areas beyond the scope of law enforcement.'[48] Yet the strategy offers only the naive assumption that enhancing ability can manufacture will: 'increased military and law enforcement capability . . . can strengthen a country's national will to initiate and sustain counternarcotics programs.' In fact, such increased capability will make corruption more profitable and increase the efficiency of enforcement agencies in taking advantage of it.

Will and Capability: The Andean Peasant Producers

The success of the US drug strategy is conditioned not only on the will and ability of political elites and institutions, but on the actions of vast segments of the Andean populations engaged in the cocaine economy. A second requisite for success is thus the ability of the US and the Andean governments to convince millions of people to stop growing, processing, and shipping coca products. This means transforming the current interests of Andean peasants in growing coca for its high profitability relative to other crops. The 'new' Andean strategy relies on the same 'carrot' and 'stick' approach that has long underpinned failed US efforts in the region.

The 'carrots' are incentives to substitute other crops for coca. The Agency for International Development (AID) 'carrot' is a four-part programme of macro-level economic assistance, alternative development and income substitution, narcotics awareness and education, and administration of justice.[49] Research is conducted to identify potential new crops, and seeds are distributed to encourage crop substitution. Farmers are trained in new production techniques and offered agricultural extension services to help them shift from coca to licit crops. Roads are repaired for easier access to markets, and broader development programmes are initiated.

The enforcement 'stick' seeks to raise the risks and costs of illegal coca growing and processing activities. The coercion includes crop eradication, interdiction of coca products, and destruction of processing labs. Over the past decade, countless hillsides of coca have been uprooted and burned or sprayed with chemical herbicides. Thousands of peasant coca-processing pits and small labs have been located and dismantled, and large quantities of coca paste and base have been seized before reaching the traffickers.

While these strategies have eliminated quantities of coca under production or in processing, they have failed to stem the increase in overall acreage under cultivation and coca paste or base produced. Despite periodic price swings, the profits to be gained from growing, processing, and transporting coca products have remained far higher than the economic alternatives.

American officials concede the failure of Andean crop substitution programs: in Peru, for example, $25 million has been invested in the Upper Huallaga Valley over a decade, with no signs of success.[50] Representative Lawrence Smith (Democrat, Florida) stated flatly, 'We have put a lot of money into crop substitution and it has gone absolutely nowhere over the past ten years.'[51]

Washington's response to the record of failure has been to change the emphasis but escalate the strategy. In recent years US drug strategists have largely abandoned the difficult and time-consuming process of forcible manual eradication of coca crops, for example, in favour of seedbed destruction and 'voluntary' eradication programs. Rather than targeting processing pits, the US has set its sights on increased lab destruction. Rhetorical and financial support for the economic assistance 'carrot' is also mounting in Washington. Efforts at local economic development, credit, and crop substitution are particularly attractive for Congressional critics looking for a less dangerous and costly alternative to militarisation of the drug war. Economic assistance may be good for the people of the region, but as an effective instrument of drug supply reduction it is chimerical, doomed by the very logic of coca production in the Andean context.

Consider the market logic from a peasant's perspective. Coca often brings *ten times* the price of competing crops. It is a hardy deep-rooted, woody bush which will produce alkaloid-bearing leaves four to six times a year for 10 to 15 years. Easy to harvest and process into paste, coca does not require transport to distant markets: traffickers (often from Colombia) fly into remote airstrips regularly and pay peasants up front in dollars. Government intervention in the market to raise the risks of coca growing and the attraction of economic alternatives are unlikely to change this logic; and localised, short-term successes do nothing to affect the rationale of other peasants – other regions or other countries – who may choose to enter the lucrative market. Consequently, neither the crop substitution carrot nor the enforcement stick can fundamentally transform the rational interests that poor peasants have in producing a high profit crop that is easy to grow and market.

The problem is illustrated by the early results of Bolivia's voluntary crop eradication and substitution program – lauded by US officials and supported by US assistance. The programme offers coca growers $2,000 per hectare for voluntarily eradicating their coca crops, and has attracted growing numbers of coca farmers. But many farmers have responded to this attractive offer by destroying only part of their coca crop, however, keeping other land planted in coca or even planting coca on new sites to ensure that they can continue to reap the benefits of the programme[52]

AID officials acknowledge the impossibility of defying the logic of the market as long as profits are high:

> Given ecology of the coca-growing regions, most viable alternative crops are tree crops such as coffee, citrus, macadamia nuts and

cacao, which only begin to produce income to the farmers several years after they are planted. Furthermore, the capacity of existing farm extension networks and banking institutions to deliver technological packages and credit to farmers is limited . . . No single crop can approach the returns from coca production at current prices, and coca growers may suffer short-term income losses as they move into legitimate occupations.[53]

When faced with evidence of such market logic, some US officials counter that 'efforts to provide alternative crops and incomes cannot succeed unless there is sustained and effective enforcement and inter- diction – activities which drive the price of coca down towards its production cost.'[54] Yet the very lack of official will and ability discussed earlier will thwart all but the most temporary and ephemeral efforts to keep coca prices down.

The ineffectiveness of enforcement measures are compounded by political obstacles. Peasants, for example, have actively resisted eradi- cation efforts, through strikes and blockades and at times through armed resistance. At least twice in early 1990, Peruvian police and DEA agents were stoned by peasants during interdiction operations. In Bolivia, coca farmers represent the most formidable organised labour force in the country; the government is reluctant to move against the coca growers federation.

Perhaps more importantly, peasants have developed counter-strategies to circumvent enforcement efforts. Growers scale down and hide crops, or replant in new regions often previously untouched by the crop. Processors reduce the size of labs, camouflage them and relocate them to more remote areas. DEA officials confirm that Peruvian producers and refiners responded to intensified counter-narcotics operations in 1989 by reconstructing labs to resemble houses from the air, relocating them farther north in the Upper Huallaga Valley, where they reportedly receive protection from complicit military officials.[55]

Panama: A Counter Case?

If the above analysis raises serious questions about the clarity of mission and whether US military force can achieve 'decisive results using decisive means' then the case of Panama might seem to provide an important counter example. In Panama, a military dictator, General Manuel Noriega, who controlled much of the country's drug trade, was overthrown in December 1989 by the decisive use of US military force and the United States was able to install a government that had previously been denied office when Noriega had rigged elections.

But what has been the consequence of what then US Ambassador to Panama Dean Hinton called 'the biggest drug bust in history'? The current volume of drug traffic now exceeds that under Noriega. A July 1991 report by the GAO concludes that drug trafficking in Panama 'may have doubled' and that money laundering – the depositing of illicit profits from trafficking in secret accounts in legitimate banks – has 'flourished.'

Panama's 1,700 miles of coastline and 1,500 islands make it a smuggler's heaven and Captain José R. Rosas, the commander of Panama's National Maritime Service (equivalent to the US Coast Guard) admitted that 'lots of drugs are coming in. The boats operate all day long, day and night.' US officials point to the seizures of increasingly large quantities of cocaine as evidence the policy is working, but Rodrigo Arosemena, head of the customs service, says that 10 kilograms of cocaine pass undetected for each kilogram seized. And American officials believe that as much as a half a ton of cocaine still flows daily through Panama, mainly en route to the US.

Despite enormous US pressure (like withholding much needed aid), the government has been unwilling to pass legislation that could stop the money laundering. A compromise bill passed in March 1991 does open up bank records to US investigators but depositors can still conceal their true identities behind the dark veil of Panama's corporation laws. In August 1991 a US Treasury official said that 'a high level of money laundering activity' appears to be continuing.[56]

Why is the drug war in Panama failing? Some Panamanian officials, anxious for more US dollars to build up the new police force cite lack of equipment and training as the major problem. Gonzalo Menendez, chief of the Public Force, said that 'If Mr Bob Martinez [then head of the Office of National Drug Policy in Washington] and all the anti-drug forces want to fight drugs they must supply the resources to the Panamanian Govenment.' More aid and training would probably make these forces more efficient, but the fundamental problem is not capability but will: the new Panamanian government and police force do not really want to fight the US drug war any more than Washington's supposed drug war 'allies' in the Andean countries of Peru, Colombia and Bolivia – and for two good reasons.

First, it is not a national priority. The new govenment inherited a $6 billion dollar foreign debt and an economy crippled by two years of US sanctions and an invasion. Unemployment stands at about 25 per cent and millions are needed to rebuild the economy. The judicial system is in chaos. Fighting the drug trade is just not that important. In fact, it could be detrimental to economic recovery. The much needed foreign dollars filtering back into Panama's 120 banks (deposits have gone from $12 billion at the time of the invasion to over $16 billion) is as one senior government lawyer frankly admitted 'drug money'.[57] So closing loopholes which allow money laundering does not make economic sense.

Second, there are high profits to be made for official collaboration with traffickers. One explanation for the Panamanian government's unwillingness to close loopholes in banking laws is the widely reputed link of senior officials to the laundering operations. President Guillermo Endara's law partner represented companies run by drug traffickers; Vice President Guillermo Ford is part owner of a bank the US Federal Bureau of Investigation has identified as a repository for Medellín drug cartel money; the attorney general was director of a bank owned by leaders of the Cali cocaine cartel; and the chief justice of the Supreme Court and the treasury minister were also members of its board.

The very US military success in Panama thus raises serious questions about a militarised drug war strategy: if the US cannot exercise its will in Panama, where it set up the government, why is there any reason to expect that governments elsewhere in Latin America will want to seriously fight its drug war?

Finding the 'Centre of Gravity' Given the 'Ballon Effect'

Clausewitz emphasises the importance to military success of finding the enemy's 'centre of gravity' – 'the hub of all power and movement upon which everything depends . . . The point against which all energies should be directed.'[58] What this centre is varies by country and conflict: it could be the enemy's *'army'*, or *'the capital'*, or *'the army of their protector'*; 'among alliances, it lies in the *community of interest*, and in popular uprisings it is the *personalities of the leaders and public opinion.'*[59] Clausewitz's sound reasoning here should raise yet another alarm bell in thinking about US military involvement in the war against Latin American drug supply: there is no 'centre of gravity'. The proliferation of the Panamanian drug trade after Noriega's overthrow should make this clear. Yet those who would persist in supporting such military solutions as a 'simultaneous (regional) attack to impact the cartel's entire support structure' – a plan *Newsweek* magazine once claimed was being considered by the US Southern Command under General Maxwell D. Thurman[60] – need to consider two further factors.

One is that the role of the cartels in the drug trade is like the role of major corporations in an oligopolistic market: a handful of corporations exercising great control over market structure and behaviour through their control over barriers to entry (economies of scale, marketing channels, etc). Busting up the cartels, like trust busting, would break the oligopoly. Yet the result would likely be a freer market in drugs (something like what happened in post-Noriega Panama) and that is not going to have a major long term impact on cutting supply and raising price in the US. One of the prime reasons why it is so difficult to find the 'drug enemy's' centre of gravity is that to a great extent the enemy is a market of hundreds of thousands of peasant producers, processors, runners, traffickers, and managers who are responding to the high profits of a large market in North America and Europe.

A second factor is that 'successful' enforcement in one area causes – and even creates incentives for – production and processing to pop up in another, like squeezing a balloon. The result is that even limited success in the drug war assures that there will never be a 'centre of gravity' since the strategy itself ultimately exacerbates the very problem it tries to solve as it encourages the dramatic spread of coca production. There is already much evidence that enforcement strategies have created an ever-widening game of cat-and-mouse in the region, as the militarisation of the drug war in the Andean countries has spread the drug trade across borders to Brazil, Ecuador, Venezuela, and Argentina.[61] 'It's like hitting mercury with a hammer', said a State Department official who deals with drug policy.[62] A February 1992 report of the House Subcommittee on Crime and Criminal Justice observed:

> Unintentionally, US enforcement efforts have hastened this spread [of the cocaine trade]. The crackdown in southern Florida shifted smuggling routes through Mexico and across the Southwest border. Pinching northbound traffic through Colombia forced the opening of new avenues southbound through Chile and Argentina. . . . When traffickers modify their methods, the Administration deems it a triumph. The fact that drug trafficking – along with corruption, violence, and addiction – has spread to an area that was previously unscathed is dismissed as irony.[63]

Hitting the mercurial centre of gravity with a hammer has a long history. Colombia's efforts to eradicate marijuana production in the late 1970s had considerable success, but the result was the expansion of production to Mexico. Mexico's campaign against marijuana production encouraged the rapid growth of production in the US (it now meets one third of domestic demand). Similarly, the breaking of the 'French connection' in heroin in the early 1970s led to the transfer of large-scale opium poppy production from Turkey to Mexico.[64]

The simple but powerful market logic of guaranteed high prices for cocaine in vast American and European markets, within a Third World context of desperate need, is, finally, the deepest force undermining local will and ability to fight the drug war.

Conclusion

If the failure of a major military success in Panama raises serious questions about the US military mission in terms of stemming the flow of drugs, and if local successes are like hitting mercury with a hammer, then research by RAND Corporation economist Peter Reuter should raise even further questions. His work shows that even if US military efforts significantly reduced supply into the United States this would have little effect on the street price for narcotics.

The reason is that the actual costs of growing and processing coca are only a minimal part of the street price in the US. In fact, even at the point of export, the price of cocaine is still only *three to five per cent* of the price a US consumer will pay. And even the smuggling costs – from Colombia to mainland USA – account for *less than five per cent* of the retail price. This means that an incredibly successful crop eradication program that tripled the leaf price of coca would raise cocaine prices in the US by only one per cent. It means that if US interdiction programmes were to seize 50 per cent of all cocaine shipped from Colombia – an impossibly high figure – this would add less then three per cent to the retail price of cocaine in the US.[65] Mathea Falco, author of *The Making of a Drug-Free America: Programs that Work*, puts the inevitable failure of a supply side drug strategy even more simply: only 4 Boeing 747 cargo planes or 13 trailer trucks could supply US cocaine consumption for a year; the annual US demand for heroin could be met by a 20-square-mile field.[66]

Given the lack of a clear political objective to define the mission for the US military in the Latin American drug war and the evidence that the drug war will be an interminable, 'limited war' with neither decisive means nor decisive results, it is clear that military force against Latin supply is not the appropriate response to the nation's drug problems. These conclusions in turn raise serious questions about the US public support that Summers rightly argues is 'an essential condition for the conduct of military operations'.[67] Granted: the largely unnoticed involvement of US Special Forces teams in the region may not immediately raise public hackles.[68] Granted: political leaders could generate some immediate public support for sending in the military. When Bush suggested sending US troops to Colombia in 1989, one national poll indicated that 74 per cent of Americans were in favour, and 36 per cent favored sending combat forces, even if some of those soldiers might be killed.[69] Yet an extended US involvement in a never-ending limited war which lacks clear objectives, whose very failure to seriously impact on supply or price will inevitably generate calls for further escalation, whose foreign allies are often corrupt or anti-democratic or serious abusers of human rights, and whose targets are often the ordinary citizens – tens of thousands of them – involved in the growing, refining, transport, and marketing of narcotics does not bode well for sustaining the necessary public support.

The harsh reality is that there is no Andean supply-reduction strategy that can significantly lower the demand for drugs at home. The supply reduction policy defies both the logic of the market and the rational interests of governments and populations – thereby undermining local will and ability to conduct a supply-side drug war. To continue to frame the central issue as how to reduce the foreign supply at the source guarantees continued failure; and to send in the US military as a response to the failure not only diverts the military from its premier mission of national defence, but also implicates it in the failure. Lieutenant General Stephen Olmstead pointed out the dangers of saddling the military with this mission in 1988 when he was then the Pentagon's top drug policy official: 'What I find is, . . . "let's make the Army a scapegoat. We don't know the answer to the drug problem, so let's assign it to the Army and let them try and solve it." '[70]

As a nation Americans must be concerned with the drug abuse, addiction, and drug-related violence which plagues our cities. Yet the central focus must be demand at home, not supply abroad. There is no magic bullet: legalisation is no more an instant cure than militarisation. US policy must confront the fact that 90 per cent of addicts at home who seek help, are turned away at treatment centres due to lack of space at the same time that millions of dollars are wasted on anti-drug military aid to the Andean countries. Federal drug policy must also confront the hard fact that many drug dealers and users will not 'just say no to drugs' unless they have something better to say 'yes' to, such as decent jobs, decent schools, a chance for a decent life. While perhaps not as glamorous and popular as an Andean drug war, providing aid for the underdeveloped territories in America's own inner cities is desperately needed to alleviate the conditions that make drug dealing and abuse so attractive.

These problems demand a domestic-focused alternative policy based on treatment, education, and urban development. How we do so is a complex issue requiring much debate and discussion among community leaders, health officials, and policy-makers – but unlike the current discourse on drug policy, it is the right debate to engage. However, this new debate cannot even begin until we abandon the foolish and costly obsession with solving the nation's drug problem in the distant jungles of South America.

NOTES

Parts of this essay draw on previous collaborative research which appears in Peter Andreas, Eva Bertram, Morris Blachman, and Kenneth E. Sharpe, 'Dead-End Drug Wars', *Foreign Policy Magazine*, Winter 1991–92. The author is grateful to Professor James Kurth at Swarthmore College for his insights and criticisms.

1. Alexander Wilde, Testimony on Andean Drug Strategy, Subcommittee on Western Hemisphere Affairs, 26 Feb. 1991, p.6.
2. Report, 'United States Anti-Narcotics Activities in the Andean Region', Committee on Government Operations, US House of Representatives, 30 Nov. 1990, p.94.
3. US State Dept., County Report on Human Rights in Colombia, 1989, p.511.
4. Cited in Washington Office on Latin America, *Clear and Present Danger* (Washington: Oct. 1991), p.121.
5. Ibid.
6. The economic data on Bolivia are drawn from Peter R. Andreas and Kenneth E. Sharpe, 'Cocaine Politics in the Andes', *Current History* (Feb. 1992), pp.75–6.
7. Col. Harry G. Summers, Jr. [Retd.], *On Strategy II: A Critical Analysis of the Gulf War*, (NY: Dell, 1992).
8. Cited in Harry G. Summers, *On Strategy, A Critical Analysis of the Vietnam War*, (NY: Dell, 1982), p.24.
9. Harry G. Summers, 'Military presence sends wrong signal, Drug war resembles several unsuccessful missions', *Miami Herald*, 20 Sept. 1989.
10. 'Powell Delivers a Resounding No on Using Limited Force in Bosnia', *New York Times*, 28 Sept. 1992.
11. Caspar W. Weinberger, 'Our Troops Shouldn't Be Drug Cops', *Washington Post*, 22 May 1988.
12. Colin L. Powell, 'Why Generals Get Nervous', *New York Times*, 8 Oct. 1992.
13. As note 10.
14. Ibid.
15. Summers, *On Strategy II* (note 7), p.13.
16. Cited in Summers, *On Strategy II*. p.11.
17. *Clear and Present Danger* (note 4), citing Office of National Drug Control Policy, *National Drug Control Strategy*, Feb. 1991, pp.78–9.
18. 'Drug trafficking and Shinning Path activities are inextricably tied together', said Melvyn Levitsky, Asst. Secretary of State for International Narcotics Matters. 'You can't fight one without fighting the other'. Clifford Krauss, *New York Times*, 7 Aug. 1991.
19. Weinberger (note 11).
20. Nancy Lubin, 'Central Asia's Drug Bazaar', *New York Times*, 16 Nov. 1992.
21. Report, 'US Anti-Narcotics Activities in the Andean Region', (note 2) 30 Nov. 1990, p.18.
22. Ibid., p.19.
23. Paul Richter and Ronald Ostrow, 'Drug War looks Like a Long One', *Los Angeles Times*, 5 Aug. 1991, p.1.
24. 'Military is Faulted on Effort to Stem Drug Traffic', *New York Times*, 27 Sept. 1991.
25. As note 2, p.76.
26. Drug Enforcement Administration [hereinafter DEA] Review, 'Institution-Building in the Andes', 12 Dec. 1989, in Appendix to Hearings 'Operation Snowcap: Past,

Present, and Future,' Committee on Foreign Affairs, US House of Representatives, 23 May 1990, p.46.
27. As note 2, p.75.
28. DEA Review (12 Dec. 1989), pp.60–1.
29. As note 2, p.39.
30. DEA Review (12 Dec. 1989), pp.60–61.
31. As note 2, p.85.
32. Report, 'Drugs and Latin America: Economic and Political Impact and US Policy Options', Proceedings of a Seminar held by the Congressional Research Service, 26 April 1989, Select Committee on Narcotics Abuse and Control, US House of Representatives, 10 Aug. 1989, p.45.
33. As note 2, p.64.
34. Further, any successes against the Shinning Path will not translate into drug supply reduction since the guerrillas' major function is simply protecting peasant profits from rapacious drug traffickers who will still operate freely in a region where peasants will still find it rational to grow coca.
35. Report, 'Stopping the Flood of Cocaine with Operation Snowcap: Is it Working?' Committee on Govt. Ops., US House of Representatives, 14 Aug. 1990, pp.83–4.
36. DEA Review, 12 Dec. 1989, p.60.
37. Ibid.
38. As note 35, p.38
39. Ibid., p.57.
40. GAO, 1988 report, p.18 cited in note 2, p.90.
41. Report, 'The Andean Drug Strategy and the Role of the US Military', Defense Policy Panel and Investigations Subcommittee, Committee on Armed Services, US House of Representatives, Jan. 1990, p.31.
42. As note 35, p.63.
43. Simon Strong, 'Peru is Losing More than the Drug War', New York Times, 17 Feb. 1992.
44. PBS Frontline, Inside The Cartel, 22 May 1990
45. As note 2, p.91.
46. Wilde testimony (note 1).
47. DEA Review, 12 Dec. 1989, p.42.
48. As note 32, p.5.
49. Hearing, 'Overview of the Agency for International Development's Economic Assistance Strategy for the Andes and Other Programs', Committee on Foreign Affairs, US House of Representatives, 3 April 1990, p.7.
50. Ibid., pp.27–9.
51. Ibid, p.31
52. Seizing Opportunities, Report of the Inter-American Commission on Drug Policy, Inst. of the Americas and the Center for Iberian and Latin American Studies, University of California, San Diego, June 1991 p.32.
53. Testimony of Frederick W. Schieck, Acting Asst. Administrator, Bureau for Latin America and the Caribbean, AID, in Hearing, 'Cocaine Production in the Andes', Select Committee on Narcotics Abuse and Control, US House of Representatives, 7 June 1989.
54. Ibid., p.11
55. As note 2, p.37.
56. New York Times, 13 Aug. 1991.
57. International Policy Report, Center for Development Policy, Washington, DC, June 1991.
58. Cited in Summers, On Strategy, A Critical Analysis of the Vietnam War (note 8), p.177.
59. Cited in ibid.
60. 'Risky Business, As its involvement in the drug war grows, the Pentagon outlines a plan to crush the cartels', Newsweek, 16 July 1990, p.16.

61. See e.g., 'Brazil's Amazon Basin Becomes Cocaine Highway', *New York Times*, 14 April 1991; 'Ecuador Fighting to Avoid Drug Link, but Laundering of Money and Investment by Traffickers Across Borders Grow', *New York Times*, 27 Jan. 1991.
62. 'Anti-drug Effort Clogs Outside US; Bush Plan to Stop Trafficking from Latin America Nets Few Results in 2 Years', *New York Times*, 25 Nov. 1990.
63. Report, 'The Andean Initiative: Squeezing a Balloon', Subcommittee on Crime and Criminal Justice, Judiciary Committee, US House of Representatives, Feb. 1992, p.3.
64. Peter H. Smith, 'The Political Economy of Drugs', in idem (ed.), *Drug Policy in the Americas* (Boulder, CO: Westview Press, 1992), p.8.
65. As note 2, pp. 33–5.
66. Cited in 'Making America Drug Free, A New Vision of What Works', *Carnegie Quarterly* 37/3 (Summer 1992), p.1.
67. Summers, *On Strategy II* (note 7), p.13.
68. Jim Pat Mills, 'The Army's Drug War', *Army Times*, 2 Oct. 1989.
69. George C. Wilson, 'Experts Doubt Military Can Stop Flow of Drugs', *Washington Post*, 8 Sept. 1989, cited in Ted Galen Carpenter and R. Channing Rouse, 'Perilous Panacea: The Military in The Drug War', Cato Inst., Policy Analysis No.128, 15 Feb. 1990, p.7.
70. Lt. Gen. Stephen Olmstead, in 'Narcotics Interdiction and the Use of the Military: Issues for Congress', Report on a Seminar held by the Congressional Res. Service, 7 June 1988, p.13.

Sustainable Democracy in Latin America: Prospects and Problems

RICHARD L. MILLETT

At the start of the 1990s democracy seemed to be an irreversible trend in the Western Hemisphere. With the ousting of General Manuel Antonio Noriega from power in Panama (December 1989), the January 1991 election of a civilian government in Haiti, and the April 1990 victory of the opposition in Nicaragua only Cuba remained in Latin America as a clearly authoritarian government. Even the *Partido Revolucionario Institucional* (PRI) in Mexico was conceding some defeats at the state level.

Events since then have not been quite so hopeful. The September 1991 military coup in Haiti, military support for President Alberto Fujimori's April 1992 dissolution of the Congress in Peru and the two attempted coups in Venezuela (February and November 1992) have served as dramatic reminders of the fragility of democratic progress. While civil conflicts have ended in Nicaragua and El Salvador, efforts to produce similar results in Colombia, Guatemala, and Peru seem to be making little progress. Meanwhile, corruption, economic crisis, and internal feuding plague many newly-installed civilian governments. This is most notable in Brazil where evidence of pervasive corruption led to the removal of President Fernando Collor de Mello from office in December 1992, and in Nicaragua, where feuding between the executive and legislative branches has helped frustrate efforts to restart the economy. All of this raises major question about the nature and viability of Latin America's progress towards democracy. It also keeps alive the issue of potential military intervention in politics and poses difficult challenges for United States policy.

The turmoil of recent years has largely laid to rest simplistic views that creating and maintaining democracy could be achieved simply through holding relatively honest elections, installing civilian governments and preventing military coups. Electoral fraud, anti-democratic elements within the military, and Marxist-Leninist insurgencies still exist, but are no longer the greatest threats to the survival of democracy. The end of the Cold War, the creation of a global economy, and the revolution in mass communications (what Arab League Ambassador Clovis Maksoud has referred to as the CNN-ization of the world due to the impact of

Cable News Network, Atlanta) have reduced old problems, but have also helped create a host of newer obstacles to democratic development. At the same time, the installation of elected, civilian regimes has highlighted basic problems in the political, social, and economic structures of Latin America.

For reasons of organisation and simplicity, this study will divide the threats to democratic development into several broad categories. The first, and perhaps most fundamental of these is the region's own history and traditions. This category includes everything from the problems posed by languages which do not include a word which can adequately be translated as compromise and which make no distinction between policy and politics, to an Iberian heritage which placed the needs of the state above the rights of individuals.

The military is heavily influenced by an historical heritage which lacks democratic roots. The armed forces have long been autonomous institutions, comprising a virtual state within a state. Civilians governments have had limited authority over military assignments and promotions, and members of military, especially officers, have a long tradition of immunity from judgement by civilian courts. Even establishing control over military budgets has been a long, arduous, and far from totally successful struggle. Officers frequently see no contradiction between what they define as support for democracy and a fierce defence of their own institutional autonomy and privileges. Supporting democracy is defined as abstaining from interference in electoral politics and refusing to create alliances with particular parties, but does not necessarily include permitting any degree of effective civilian control over their own institutions.

In much of Hispanic America, especially in nations with large indigenous populations, the military is still the direct descendant of *el ejercito de la conquista*. Defence of the nation does not necessarily mean defence of the population, indeed the population can easily be seen as a potential enemy. High command is regarded as a reward for years of faithful service to *la patria*, carrying with it the right to use the position for personal and family advancement.

Another obstacle to democratic development is Latin America's long history of class and caste divisions. The 500th anniversary of the voyages of Christopher Columbus both underlined this heritage and contributed to the trend of indigenous peoples to organise and to challenge their subordinate place in society. In many ways, this is a positive sign of democratic development. Yet it is also a source of potential conflict and fragmentation.

If the weight of the past hampers and threatens efforts at democratic development, the demographic pressures of the present offer at least an equal challenge. The region has made notable progress in controlling population growth over the past three decades, but the issue is far from resolved. Continued population growth rates of over 2 per cent in many nations place constant burdens of governments in such areas as education and job creation. More fundamental has been the almost uncontrolled growth of urbanisation, especially to the central cities which dominate 16 of continental Latin America's 20 nations. While the region's rural population increased by just over 20 per cent from 1960 to 1990 the urban population increased 200 per cent in the same period.[1] This, in turn, has had a disastrous impact on government budgets, since the cost of services for those in urban areas is many times that for those in rural areas.

Population growth and urbanisation have contributed to the regions growing ecological crisis. This, in turn, places one more burden on democratic governments, trying to reconcile the urgent needs of the population with the necessity to preserve the environment for future generations.

These pressures contribute to the third area of obstacles to democratic consolidation, the profound social crisis. The region's per capita Gross Domestic Product declined 1.2 per cent during the 1980s, after experiencing rather steady growth for the previous two decades.[2] Taking into account the increase in urbanisation, the debt crisis, and the costs of internal conflicts the actual situation was much worse.

While the demands on governments were growing, resources were frequently shrinking. This contributed to low levels of popular approval, to deteriorating services and infrastructure, and to efforts to reduce the costs of government employment. While this last factor had a positive side, given the bloated nature of government payrolls, it also fueled discontent, especially in some sectors of the armed forces, and further contributed to inefficiency and corruption in the police.

Governments have found themselves under increasing pressure to curb inflation, privatise government industries, reduce subsidies, and curb social spending in order to reduce deficits. These austerity programmes, while often long overdue, tend to hit the poorest sectors hardest. Popular reactions against such programmes have been a major factor in recent disturbances in Venezuela, and other nations.

Centralisation of power and authority has long been a Latin American tradition. Local governments have often been mere adjuncts to central authorities, lacking power and resources. This has been a significant impediment both to democratic consolidation and to economic progress.

Recently, notable efforts have been made in several countries to reverse this longstanding trend. Direct election of local officials has resumed in Colombia and other in other countries, local governments have obtained increased powers in Mexico and Venezuela, and there have even been efforts at restoring some local controls over law enforcement.

Efforts to strengthen local governments have been seriously hampered by a lack of funds and of trained personnel. At times, the return of power to local levels also reflects the weakness of national states which lack the resources needed to deal with problems on the periphery. There is a danger that this process could produce a resurgent form of warlordism, especially in areas where narcotics trafficking offers alternative revenues, and/or where insurgent forces have long been active.

Many of the greatest problems for democratic transitions have been created by civilian politicians. One manifestation of this has been the proliferation of political parties. In over half the nations of Latin America no party has a majority in the Congress. In many cases the president's own party is not even the largest.

While the growth of new parties and the necessity of coalition building can be signs of healthy democratic development, this is often not the case. Parties frequently split over personal ambitions and rivalries. Long established parties are in a state of crisis in many areas, notably the Conservative Party in Colombia and *Action Democratica* in Venezuela. Alliances formed to win elections often collapse soon thereafter, disrupting administrative organisation and producing bitter recriminations.

The proliferation of parties contributes to a more fundamental problem, the threat of executive-legislative gridlock. North Americans may feel more than a nodding familiarity with this situation, but the United States' problems in this area pale into insignificance alongside those prevailing in some Latin American nations. Congresses have traditionally been subordinated to the executive branch in Latin America.[3] Popular support for the institution has often been low, members have often shown little interest in their constituencies, or, conversely, have been tools of local political bosses. Legislative bodies lack experience, staff, and budget. What they do not lack is personal ambitions and a growing willingness to clash with the executive branch.

The results have frequently been disastrous. In both Peru and Haiti clashes between the executive and legislative powers help precipitate military coups, in the first case in alliance with the President, in the second, in alliance with the Congress. In Nicaragua such divisions have contributed to an endemic state of political crisis and the nation now faces the possibility of having two rival congresses in existence at the same time.[4] In Panama conflicts between Congress and the executive have contributed to the government's extreme unpopularity and have provided an opening for renewed influence by the Revolutionary Democratic Party (PRD), the primary political supporter of the Noriega dictatorship.

If problems in the legislative branch can threaten the consolidation of democracy, the problem is at least as great if not greater in the legal system. Like the legislative branch, the judiciary in Latin America has little history of effective independence from executive control. In many nations the entire judicial system is run by the central government. Judges are poorly paid and trained, lack staff, and are highly vulnerable to political and economic pressures. Their task is frequently complicated by the poor quality and rampant corruption of the police, by outdated legal codes, and by spiraling crime rates. Add to these problems created by narcotics trafficking, active insurgencies, and longstanding traditions of virtual immunity for military, political, and economic elites and you have an institution which is incapable of functioning effectively. Discussing the crisis in the judiciary with the Auxiliary Bishop of Ayacucho, Peru, I asked him if he would take a case to his nation's courts. 'Absolutely not' he replied. 'I couldn't afford to buy the decision.'[5] When there is no justice available for a bishop, it is obvious that there is none for the average citizen. This situation strikes at the heart of the democratic process. If citizens whose rights are violated by the state have no potentially effective remedy for such violations, then democracy can scarcely be said to exist. If the state is unable to promote justice and defend individual rights then faith in and support for the system rapidly declines. If the civil justice system does not function, then efforts to reduce or end military immunity from prosecution for offences against civilians and to hold officers accountable for their actions are greatly hampered.

The problem of immunity and impunity applies to civilians as well as to the military. Despite the massive corruption of numerous recent governments very few high-ranking politicians have been brought to justice. Former presidents, cabinet ministers, and other government officials living in ostentatious wealth, something which they lacked before entering government, are a conspicuous sight throughout much of the hemisphere.

Under the existing system, those who are not to some extent immune are usually totally vulnerable. Those without influence, or those who for whatever reason have incurred the wrath of governments in power often have few real rights. In Panama, for example, in late 1991, 84 per cent of the prisoners in jail were still awaiting trial. Many had been in this situation for longer than the sentences for the crimes of which they were accused. Prisons were extremely overcrowded, record keeping was chaotic, and the system of public defenders hopelessly inadequate.[6] By the end of 1992 none of the major military figures arrested after the 1989 US invasion had yet been brought to trial.

Situations similar to that existing in Panama are found throughout the hemisphere. The concept that losers as well as winners have rights, fundamental to the consolidation of a democratic system, is frequently absent in Latin America. Under such a situation it is hardly to be expected that military officers or any other privileged group would willingly give up their immunities and submit themselves to such a judicial system. Until significant progress is made in this area, effective consolidation of democracy will be virtually impossible.

The weakness of the police and the crime wave affecting most large Latin American cities is also a threat to the democratic process. High levels of personal insecurity contribute to a loss of faith in the system and a willingness to embrace authoritarian alternatives. This also leads to a proliferation of private security agencies, often better armed than the police, and to forms of vigilantism. The most extreme expressions of this, such as the killing of street children in Brazil and Guatemala, accelerates the *desprestigio* of governments, damaging their international image and discrediting the entire judicial system.

In such situations, the temptation to use the military in police roles becomes almost irresistible. They are available and are already on the payroll. The long-range results, however, are often disastrous. The military resents being used in such roles. Involvement in policing operations, especially those related to the narcotics trade, increases corruption within the armed forces. Use of the military in anti-riot and other measures involving operations against the civilian population inevitably leads to human rights violations and to increased public hostility towards the armed forces. It also diverts attention and resources from the vital task of improving the police. Resentment over their use in police roles was a major factor in the February 1992 coup attempt by elements of the Venezuelan military.[7]

The pattern of civil-military relations remains an obstacle to the consolidation of the democratic process. The threat of military coups has declined over the past decade, and ability of the armed forces to dominate the political process has been significantly reduced. Political parties no longer seek open alliances with the military, military candidates generally fare poorly in elections. The armed forces have increasingly taken a neutral position in the electoral process. Yet high levels of mutual suspicions remain, communications between the military and civilians are often poor and distorted, and uncertainties over military roles, budgets, and even chains of command provide numerous points of actual and potential conflict. If the old pattern of civil-military relations in Latin America has largely broken down, no clear and consistent new pattern has yet emerged. The military is a highly traditional institution. It resists rapid change, dislikes uncertainty, and is easily persuaded that those outside the institution not only do not understand it, but are at least potentially hostile to it. Such attitudes contributed to the coups in Peru and Haiti, to the coup attempts in Venezuela, and have dangerous implications for the democratic process in several other nations.

Military support for democracy is an essential element of a successful democratic transition. Two primary elements in achieving and maintaining such support are clear definitions of military roles and missions and consistent, effective systems for establishing civilian control over the armed forces. Traditional military roles such as defending the national territory against external aggression and dealing with internal insurgencies are of diminishing importance. The international political and economic climate makes conventional wars in the hemisphere unlikely. As the Falklands/Malvinas conflict and the 1991 Gulf War demonstrated, attempts to solve territorial disputes, the leading cause of wars in Latin American history, by force are simply too costly and too risky to be worth attempting. The loss of international support for insurgencies which accompanied the end of the Cold War has led to a decline in the number and level of these conflicts. As previously noted, use of the military in police-type functions, especially in the control of civil disturbances, runs high risks.

Other potential missions such as defence of the environment and internal development efforts can produce jurisdictional and budgetary conflicts with civilian agencies of the government. Only peacekeeping provides a clear, new mission for the military, and this can involve only a small percentage of the existing force. In the coming decade the region's armed forces will face increasing pressures to reduce both their strength and their share of the budget. If such efforts are to succeed there will have to be careful plans for retraining both officers and enlisted men for other careers. While some missions such as environmental protection and anti-narcotics activity might best be undertaken by new organisations, separate from the armed forces, the assignment of personnel from the military to these units could reduce the burdens and dangers of the force reduction process.

In such situations, it is critical to maintain clear, consistent, and effective lines of civilian control over the military. Colombia's recent decision in install a civilian defence minister is an important step in that direction. The creation of civilian staffs, competent in military matters, but loyal to and dependent on civilian superiors is vital. So, too, is the creation and empowerment of congressional committees dealing with defence-related matters. Programmes of joint civil-military education, such as Guatemala's Centro ESTNA, can play a vital role in preparing civilian leadership and in establishing communication between civilians and the military.[8]

Perhaps the greatest threat to the democratic process is the high level of corruption which has been a major factor in the coup attempts in Venezuela. Similar scandals have plagued other governments in recent years. Official corruption contributed to the discrediting of Christian Democratic governments in Guatemala and El Salvador, to a presidential suicide in the Dominican Republic, and to the impeachment of President Collor de Mello in Brazil. Allegations of rampant corruption in the military are currently major issues in many nations, notably Paraguay, Honduras, and Nicaragua.

Corruption hinders economic growth, increases government inefficiency, undermines public confidence and support, and exacerbates problems in areas such as civil-military relations and judicial reform. Promises to deal with it are frequent, results are much rarer, leading to public anger and cynicism.

With all these problems, prospects for democratic consolidation in the hemisphere may appear weak indeed. In some ways, the situation seems reminiscent of that which prevailed in the late 1950s and early 1960s. Then, books such as John J. Johnson's *Political Change in Latin America: The Emergence of the Middle Sectors*, and Tad Szulc's *Twilight of the Tyrants* proclaimed that Latin America was entering a period of fundamental transition towards more democratic systems. These hopes, however, proved illusory. Within less than a decade military dictatorships, not democratic governments, were the prevailing model in the hemisphere and human rights violations were climbing to new heights.

There is reason, however, to believe that today's situation is fundamentally different from that prevailing 30 years ago. Both the international political and economic climate militate against any return to earlier patterns of authoritarian rule. The end of the Cold War significantly reduced the threat from the left to democratic institutions and made external forces less willing to accept, much less support, repressive regimes. Far from seeing such governments as potential allies in the international arena, they are now viewed, especially by the United States, as dangerous and disruptive, threatening both to economic and political interests.

The Latin American nations, themselves, show signs of becoming effectively united in the defence of democratic institutions. Such efforts, hampered by longstanding concerns over external interventions in domestic politics, still have a long way to go. But, aided by a resurgent Organization of American States, they have contributed to the holding of free elections in Nicaragua, Guyana, and El Salvador and to the isolation of the regimes in Haiti and Cuba. Concerted action within the hemisphere pressured the Fujimori administration in Peru into some concessions, and has discouraged support for coup attempts in Venezuela and elsewhere.

The revolution in communications have made it all but impossible for governments to violate the rights of their citizens with impunity. International pressure led to the trial of the officers involved with the Jesuit murders in El Salvador. The awarding of the 1992 Nobel Peace Prize to Rigoberta Menchú has focused world attention on the situation of the indigenous population of Guatemala. Popular pressures led to the trials of officers involved in Argentina's dirty war of the 1970s and may produce similar results in Brazil. While the future is uncertain, a return to patterns of repression of the past seems improbable.

Although some officers cling to the practices and values of the past, the bulk of the military exhibits little interest in or support for efforts to resurrect the pattern of military rule of the 1960s and 1970s. The experiences of this period left the armed forces badly burned. Institutional military rule produced divisions within the military, led to a loss of prestige and to international isolation, proved disastrous for efforts at economic development, and often exacerbated rather than resolved sources of domestic conflict. While still distrustful of civilian politicians, most officers neither want nor feel obligated to take on the responsibilities of governing their nations.

This does not mean, however, that the democratic transition is by any means secure. While coups are no longer seen as a desirable or logical option, they may still be seen in times of crisis as the least awful alternative available. While internal repression carries with it much greater risks and costs than in previous eras it is always an available option which can be used by those who feel their hold on power threatened.

Periods of major political transition are always fraught with danger. The failure of efforts at democratic transitions in revolutionary France produced first the Terror and then the reign of Napoleon. The failure of democratic transition in post-World War I Germany produced, through the electoral process, the rule of Adolf Hitler. The failure of democratic transitions following Spanish America's independence led to the despair of Simon Bolivar (died 1830), the chaotic dictatorships of Antonio López de Santa Ana in Mexico (1833–55), and the civil conflicts of the Juan Manuel de Rosas era in Argentina (1829–52). If transitions to democracy offer great opportunities, their failures can produce situations even worse than those which preceded the democratic experiments.

Today, the greatest threat to democracy comes not from the military, not from domestic radicals, not from foreign interventions, but from the potential loss of faith in the process by a nation's own population. Despair, fuelled by mounting economic and social problems, by government gridlock and rampant corruption undermines efforts at democratic consolidation. Frustration with a paralysed legal system, combined with rising levels of personal insecurity makes citizens willing to consider a return to patterns of official repression.

The current situation in Venezuela provides a clear warning of the dangers of popular frustration and despair. In responding to the first coup attempt (February 1992), former President Rafael Caldera commented:

> The coup is reprehensible and deplorable in every way, but it would be naive to think that it is just a matter of the adventures of a few ambitious individuals who acted precipitously on their own without thinking what they were getting into. This is an ambiènce, a groundswell, a perilous situation in the country and if that situation is not confronted, many very serious problems lie ahead of us.[9]

The warning of ex-President Caldera applies not only to Venezuela, but also to most of Latin America. Latin America today has a real chance to break the cycles of repression, dictatorship, and civil conflict which have characterised much of its history. Yet if both civilian and military leaders persist in the practices which have discredited themselves and their institutions and contributed to public despair, and if the larger international community is unable or unwilling to help the region deal with its pressing social and economic problems then the movement towards democracy may prove unsustainable. If that happens then the citizens of Latin America, like those of Germany in the 1930s, may find themselves in a much worse situation than that which preceded their efforts to create truly democratic institutions.

NOTES

1. Inter-American Development Bank, *Economic and Social Progress in Latin America, 1991 Report*, (Washington, DC: Inter-American Development Bank, 1991), p.272
2. Ibid. p.273.
3. Chile has been something of an exception to this rule.
4. The current issue revolves around a conflict between the Sandinista-controlled Supreme Court and the National Assembly, but the root issue is the split between the government of President Violeta Barios de Chamorro and the coalition of parties which supported her election in 1990.
5. Interview with Auxiliary Bishop of Ayacucho, Peru, May 1991.
6. General Accounting Office, *Aid to Panama: Improving the Criminal Justice System* (GAO/NSIAD-92-147, May 1992), pp.6–8.
7. *New York Times*, 7 Feb., 1992, p.A3. Foreign Broadcast Information Service [FBIS], *Latin America: Daily Report*, 28 Feb. 1992. p.44: 29 June 1992, pp.41–42..
8. The Centro ESTNA (Center for the Study of National Stability) is an educational project for both military and civilians in Guatemala. Supported by USAID funds and by contributions from Guatemala's private sector, it runs an annual course for representatives of the armed forces, government agencies, political parties, labour, religious and business groups, and representatives of the nation's indigenous population. Its programme of speakers and readings focuses attention on both regional and national developments, and encourages analysis and discussion of national problems.
9. FBIS, 2 March 1992, p.56.

Democratisation and Human Rights: Implication of the Latin American Experience for US Global Policy

HOWARD J. WIARDA

The movement in the last 15 years of many Latin American and other countries towards democracy, and the impetus and applause that US policy has given to this movement, should not blind us to the very real difficulties accompanying a pro-democracy, pro-human rights policy. By this time there is near-universal, even bipartisan, support for a democratisation/human rights policy, but it has not always been so. Democracy and human rights are now right up there with God, apple pie, and motherhood (assuming that we still support all *those* institutions!); no one (and certainly not this author) could be opposed to them. But while the democracy/human rights agenda has provided a marvellous opportunity for US foreign policy, it also has the potential to be a trap as well. We need to explore how and why this may be so, and to be apprised of the pitfalls.

Latin America has been the main venue, the living laboratory, where the US experimental policies in support of democracy and human rights were first tried out. But now the policy has become a global one encompassing Russia, Eastern Europe, the former Soviet republics, China, Africa, and maybe even the Middle East. As the US attempts to pursue a global foreign policy in support of democracy and human rights, it needs to keep in mind both the warning lights that continue to flash from the Latin American experience, as well as the go-ahead signs. We need to be aware of the sensitivities, the flashpoints, and the policy dilemmas involved in the democracy/human rights policy, as well as the promises.

The issue is particularly acute as the United States armed forces are now increasingly involved in democracy-building programmes. On one level, the end of the Cold War implies that such non-traditional defence and security issues as democracy and human rights will receive greater attention from defence planners. On another level, democracy and human rights are often viewed at high political levels in the Pentagon as a way, like counter-narcotics, of continuing to justify military budgets and missions. At still a third level, the Defense Department – like other agencies--has been directed to support and enhance a pro-democracy/ human rights foreign policy, in El Salvador and elsewhere. All of these pressures make it incumbent that policy planners on both the defence and civilian side understand clearly the history and unresolved dilemmas of this policy, as well as its obvious advantages.

History

The United States has, in a sense, always had a foreign policy grounded on democracy and human rights. The United States achieved its independence from Britain on the basis of its struggle for representative self-government; we sympathised with the ideals of liberty, equality, and fraternity of the French Revolution; and most Americans supported the efforts of Latin America to achieve independence and democracy in the early nineteenth century. The United States 'liberated' Texas as well as the American Southwest from Mexico in the name of democracy, fought Spain in 1898 to bring freedom to Cuba, sent the Marines to numerous spots in the Caribbean in the early twentieth century to bring the presumed benefits of democracy to, as President William H. Traft put it, our 'little brown and black brothers', and of course President Woodrow Wilson involved the US in World War I in order to 'make the world safe for democracy'. Diplomatic historians have been quick to point out that democracy was not always the real goal let alone the outcome in all of these cases,[1] but the US ethos and history have nonetheless led the nation more or less consistently to justify its policies in terms of seeking democratic ends.

Critics of this emphasis – Hans Morgenthau, George Kennan, and Henry Kissinger – have urged the US to eschew moralism in its policy and to embrace a policy based on realism and the national interest. The debate waxed in the 1950s, 1960s and 1970s. On the one side stood the idealists who argued that the US was a special nation, a 'city on a hill', a case of 'exceptionalism'. It was, they argued, America's duty and moral responsibility to provide leadership in an amoral world, to set an example, to stand firmly for our ideals of freedom and democracy. On the other side were the realists who advocated a hard-headed and pragmatic foreign policy, free of moral restraints; as one realist put it, 'we have no friends in the world, only interests.'[2]

As part of the Alliance for Progress, John F. Kennedy had supported new democratic openings in Latin America. His administration had even tried for a time to stem the wave of military-authoritarian takeovers that began to occur in the early 1960s. Yet these efforts were insufficient to hold back authoritarianism. In fact, when faced with the choice, at the height of the Cold War, between a weak and often wobbly Latin American democrat who might allow full freedom for the left *and* a strong, authoritarian regime that vigorously pursued anti-communism, the Kennedy and Johnson administrations invariably chose the strong authoritarian over the wobbly democrat. The policy was known, somewhat derisively, as the 'lesser evil doctrine'.

It was during this period of seeming US preference for authoritarians, coupled of course with the Vietnam War protests, that a manifest human rights lobby and policy-in-preparation began to be formed. It is to be emphasised that this was different from the typical, historic, and generalised American *preference* in support of democracy abroad; this was a narrower group, a lobby, a political point of view with a specific policy position. And therein lay the first problem with US human rights policy: it was not entirely clear if human rights and democracy were really the agenda or was it a particular and partisan political agenda whose aim was to use the human rights issue for other purposes?[3]

The answer to that question is unclear, and will probably always remain so. The impetus to Congress on human rights issues during this period of the late 1960s came from an amorphous coalition known as the 'human rights movement' or 'community'. The movement's activities were coordinated by the Human Rights Working Group of the Coalition for a New Foreign and Military Policy, which was headed by anti-Vietnam war activists. The movement brought together a variety of anti-war groups, including the innocuous-sounding Clergy and Laity Concerned; its ranks included such anti-war and left-wing stalwarts as Jane Fonda, Tom Hayden, Jacqui Chagnon, Staughton Lynd, and Ramsey Clark. The driving force within the movement was the peace groups as well as the New Left and the Old Left. In Congress these groups found sympathetic ears among such persons as Senator Tom Harkin, Congressman Ron Dellums, and the left wing of the Democratic Party. Within the movement – and that is what makes our interpretation difficult – were numerous people (clergy, students, citizens) who genuinely wanted to promote human rights. Yet others wanted to use the human rights issue to promote their own, generally left-wing political agenda. These 'other agendas' of several groups that call themselves human rights defenders remain a part of the problem of human rights policy still today – even though the essentials of the human rights policy have by now been incorporated and coopted into official US policy.[4]

The first legislation systematically linking US foreign policy to human rights issues was the Jackson-Vanik amendment to the 1972 trade agreement with the Soviet Union, which tied trade concessions to greater opportunities for dissidents to emigrate. In the next four years other pieces of legislation were put in place making US bilateral assistance conditional on the recipients' human rights performance. Efforts were also made to extend human rights 'conditionality' to the major international lending agencies such as the World Bank.

The policy was controversial from the beginning and was strongly opposed by the White House, the State Department, and then National Security Adviser, Henry Kissinger. Presidents Richard Nixon and Gerald Ford opposed the policy as constituting unwanted and unwarranted congressional interference in their foreign policy-making prerogatives. The State Department took the position that human rights were a domestic matter of the countries with which Washington had relations and in which the US ought not to interfere. Kissinger saw the policy from his *realpolitik* perspective as causing potentially immense problems for his budding balance-of-power policy in such important (and human rights-abusing) countries as China, Iran, the Soviet Union, Brazil, and the Philippines. The debate was fierce; but through the mid-1970s, while the legislation calling for human rights observance continued gradually to expand, the White House and State were still able generally to pursue their grand strategies without the constraints of a body of human rights restrictions.

All of this changed under President Jimmy Carter. During the 1976 campaign, but especially in his May 1977 speech at Notre Dame University (Indiana), Carter elevated human rights into *the* number one priority of his administration. His transition team at the State Department brought in several officials at the assistant secretary and deputy assistant secretary levels who were recruited out of the human rights movement. In addition, at the deputy assistant secretary level, and on the policy planning staff were some key but often lower level and therefore obscure individuals from the anti-war, McGovern, left-wing of the Democrat Party and who were strongly committed to the causes, including human rights, of 'the movement'. Carter did not closely supervise appointments below the cabinet level so a significant number of persons were recruited into his administration who emerged from what were considered fringe movements of the 1960s but who now were in charge of official policy.

The institutional apparatus for a vigorous human rights policy was also put in place. At State, what had been an 'office' of human rights was now elevated into a full-fledged 'bureau'. Pat Derian, a former civil rights activist in the US South who thought that that noble but particular struggle could be carried over into other cultures and societies, was made Assistant Secretary for Human Rights and Humanitarian Affairs. Increasingly, policy in various regional areas had to be in conformity with the norms laid down by the human rights bureau. When there were conflicts between the regional bureau (such as for Latin America) and the human rights bureau, the dispute was settled by a special committee leaded by then–Deputy Secretary of State Warren Christopher. Invariably, the Christopher committee sided with the human rights bureau and against the regional bureaus who, after all, knew far better the circumstances in the individual areas or countries of dispute.

The Carter foreign policy record and failures are too well known to be discussed at length here. These include Iran, where the Carter human rights policy helped undermine the Shah and led to the Ayatollah Khomeini, Islamic fundamentalism, and the imprisonment of the US Embassy hostages. The cases include the important South American countries of Argentina, Brazil, and Chile, then governed under military regimes but in which historic close relations with the US were sacrificed for the sake of a futile and self-defeating human rights policy. Derian's approach in dealing with these critical countries was to rant and rave and condemn the entire nation or its armed forces as 'fascist' (as distinct from condemning the individual bad apples in it), thus forcing the rest of the population to defend the regime or the rest of the officers to defend the military institution on nationalistic grounds. Another case was Nicaragua where, as Professor Anthony Lake showed, the Carter administration was torn between its desire for human rights and its (contradictory) unwillingness to sanction intervention, which resulted in disastrous indecision and temporising thus enabling the Sandinistas both to seize power and to consolidate their hold on power while progressively excluding other, democratic groups.[5]

In long-range terms (but of course in the long run, as John Maynard Keynes said, we are all dead), Carter's human rights policy did help undermine the legitimacy of these authoritarian regimes and helped lead to the re-establishment of democracy. In short-range terms, however (other than a handful of people being released from jail), the policy was a disaster. Not only did it not improve the human rights situation in these countries but it hardened the resolve of the military regimes to stay in power and to resist Washington's pressures. Moreover it produced such strong anti-American sentiment in these countries that it led to a permanent estrangement which, despite the surface manifestations of agreement on open markets and democracy, has not fully healed to this day. From this point on, in contrast to the previous 150 years of history that had even in its darkest moments at least paid lip service to the pan-American ideal of hemisphere cooperation, the two parts of the hemisphere, North and South, seemed destined to go permanently in their own separate, distinct directions. Hence despite some notable diplomatic accords over Panama and Israeli-Egyptian relations – both of which look increasingly threadbare as time goes on – the Carter presidency is almost universally thought of by the experts as a foreign policy failure.[6]

The Carter human rights policy was very controversial and came under strong attack from presidential candidate Ronald Reagan and his foreign policy advisers during the 1976 campaign. The Reagan people accused Carter of having 'lost' Iran, Nicaragua, Afghanistan, Ethiopia, Grenada, Angola, Mozambique, and perhaps El Salvador, Guatemala and others during his watch. They blamed the Carter human rights policy for helping to lose most of these nations to Marxism-Leninism since the Carter policy had undermined erstwhile allies (however tyrannical) and paved the way for takeovers by parties hostile to the United States.[7] It should be emphasised, since the point is frequently misunderstood, that the criticisms were not against human rights *per se* ('What else do we stand for if not democracy and human rights?' Reagan UN Ambassador Jeane Kirkpatrick and a strong Carter critic once rhetorically asked the author). Rather, the criticism centred on the following points:[8]

(1) Carter's elevation of human rights to a position of virtually the *only* consideration in US foreign policy, to the exclusion of economic, commercial, diplomatic, security, and military interests.

(2) The double standard involved; right wing regimes who were allies of the US were picked on far more than left wing regimes such as the Soviet Union or Cuba who constituted the real threat to US interests.

(3) The policy was applied inconsistently, incoherently, and with no agreed-upon criteria; even the definition of 'human' rights was changed several times.

(4) The persons charged with carrying out the policy were often incompetent and knew appallingly little about the countries where the policy was applied.

(5) The policy was unsophisticated and indiscriminating; it used too blunt instruments; and it was unable to distinguish between the often mild repression practised by authoritarian regimes and the massive abuses of communist regimes.

(6) The policy was often counterproductive for the reasons already indicated; it led frequently to a hardening of attitudes rather than to much reform.

(7) The policy was unrealistic. It could not sort out the possible from the merely desirable or the desirable from the impossible. It often verged on the romantic and wishful rather than having a strong base in international realities.

(8) The policy was ineffective in terms of human rights goals. It produced few changes. A few people were helped but basic policy in the offending countries was unchanged. There was a lot of noise over very little.

The Reagan administration was determined to change this orientation. However, the administration was not monolithic on the issue: not only were there different points of view but the administration also changed dramatically over time.

Some of the Reagan foreign policy team were so exorcised by the Carter human rights policy that they were determined to abolish it. For example, Reagan's first nominee for the post of Assistant Secretary for Human Rights and Humanitarian Affairs, Ernest LeFever, avowed that, if confirmed, he would abolish the very office for which he was being considered. It was not that LeFever was against human rights; in fact he had a long history as a fierce human rights activist. But he believed human rights was a domestic issue of each country and should have no place in foreign policy. LeFever, however, failed to win Senate confirmation; meanwhile cooler heads and a different view began to prevail.

In spring 1981 and continuing into 1982 two themes began to come together. The first was a new view of human rights policy in general. the reasoning, quite different from the Carter approach, was as follows:

(1) There is a close relationship between democracy and human rights. Democratic governments are more likely to respect human rights, and therefore a policy in favor of democracy is also in favour of human rights.

(2) There is a close relationship between Soviet expansionism and the loss of human rights. There is also a close relationship between US/Western influence and the protection of human rights. Therefore a policy of opposition to Soviet expansionism and of strengthening the US is also a pro-human rights policy.

(3) The US must sometimes work with friendly authoritarian regimes that are resisting communism. Because such regimes can be nudged toward democracy, and because a communist takeover will make human rights even worse, that is also a pro-human rights stance.

(4) A government (like Cuba's) that provides some social and economic benefits but denies basic political and human rights is not a pro-human rights regime.

This was obviously a Cold War/ideological position that could be used to berate the Soviet Union and its allies. Yet meanwhile, second, on the ground, another case was being decided that would have a profound effect on US human rights policy: El Salvador. The El Salvador case provided not theoretical arguments as above, but hard-headed practical lessons about the political consequences of human rights. We cannot review all of this history here but recall that in 1981 US policy in El Salvador was on the ropes, faced with the unhappy choice between allowing the Marxist guerrillas to triumph, which was clearly unacceptable to the goal of preventing 'another Cuba' or 'another Nicaragua' in the region, and supporting an exceedingly repressive military regime that raped and murdered nuns and many others, which was clearly unacceptable from a moral and a domestic politics viewpoint. Hence the US helped engineer a series of elections and reforms which eventually brought moderate, democratic, civilian, elected Christian-Democrat José Napoleon Duarte to power, and thus gave a third and quite attractive alternative to the unacceptable other two.

Out of this experience Washington learned some critical lessons which it then applied to other countries and to human rights policy in general:

(1) The Congress will support the policy if you stand for promoting democracy instead of allying with a repressive military.

(2) Ditto the media

(3) Ditto the religious groups and human rights lobbies

(4) Ditto the public

(5) Ditto our allies

(6) Standing for human rights and democracy gives unity and justifiable purpose to the government and the diverse foreign policy bureaucracies.

(7) Democratic governments do not start stupid wars that cause us no end of trouble, à la Argentina in the Malvinas/ Falklands.

(8) Democratic governments do not (à la Nicaragua) aid guerrilla campaigns in other people's countries.

(9) Democratic governments do not send terrorists into neighbouring countries or seek to destabilise those countries.

(10) Democratic governments do not ally themselves with the
Soviet Union or allow themselves to be used as bases for
Soviet machinations.

(11) Democratic governments simply cause much less grief than
either right wing regimes (Somoza, Pinochet, Marcos) or left
wing ones (Cuba, Nicaragua)

A careful reading of this list reveals that these are all very *practical*
and hard-headed reasons to be in favour of human rights, not romantic
or idealistic ones. Moreover, what the Reagan administration dis-
covered – gradually, by fits and starts, and without that being planned in
advance – is that with this policy it had an opportunity to blend and fuse
both idealistic (democracy, human rights) concerns and very realistic
ones (anti-communism, defence of the national interests), and thus to
erase once and for all that historic conflict between idealism and realism
that had long bedeviled American foreign policy. The policy is both
popular domestically (who could be against democracy and human
rights?) but it is also effective internationally by helping to undermine
communist regimes and enabling the reform of authoritarian ones.
What could be better than this?[9]

It is no surprise that a policy that combined so many good things
would quickly become very popular. Both Congress and the White
House could support it. It not only 'saved' foreign policy chestnuts in El
Salvador, Guatemala, Nicaragua, Chile, and numerous other Latin
American countries, but it also helped usher in the greatest foreign
policy triumphs of the post-World War II era when both Eastern
Europe and then the Soviet Union disintegrated and moved towards
democracy. It is small wonder that this new, updated version of human
rights policy came to enjoy widespread bipartisan support; indeed the
support for this policy is so strong that it is inconceivable that any future
administration would abandon it. Bush clearly followed this revamped
Reagan policy; President Bill Clinton has done the same. There are
really no alternatives anymore.

Unresolved Dilemmas of Human Rights Policy

While it is easy to wax hyperbolic over this unaccustomed consensus on
the democracy/human rights agenda, we need to recognise the pitfalls,
limitations, and possible traps in this approach as well. American policy
pronouncements tend to slide over and avoid these problems, and just

to say 'democracy' and 'human rights' has become an incantation that by expression alone seems to leave no further doubts or room for discussion. Yet in fact things are more complicated than that; and particularly as the US military is called upon in this post-Cold War era to take on new missions including the furtherance of democracy and human rights, it needs to know the potential problems involved.

(1) *Diverse meanings of democracy and human rights.* Clearly in China, the Islamic world, and Africa, democracy has different meanings than it has in the West. Even in Latin America, which is a predominantly Western area, democracy has always been more centralised, 'organic', and Rousseauian, as contrasted with the Lockean, Madisonian version of the United States.[10] No democracy/human rights policy can be successful unless it recognises both the universals of democracy *and* the subtle differences. Not every nation can or will be forced into the US mould; rather each must adapt the universals of democracy and human rights to its own particular culture, society, and circumstances.

(2) *Distinct categories of human rights.* Human rights may be divided into three categories: torture and crimes against the person, political and civil rights (free speech, assembly, etc.), and social or economic rights (housing, health care, education, etc.). The experience so far has been that there is more global consensus on the first two of these than on the third, and therefore better chances for success. In addition, the third category is very expensive to implement and most countries have been unwilling to take up very much of the burden of paying for such 'rights' in countries other than their own.

(3) *Even-handedness.* China (as a check on the Soviet Union) and Saudi Arabia (oil) have long been considered so important that they have largely been exempted from human rights considerations. But with the end of the Cold War China seems no longer to be free from criticism. Besides Saudi Arabia and Kuwait, are there other nations of such overriding importance that we should not pay their human rights blemishes any attention? How about Mexico, which is certainly not democratic by US standards but lies right on America's border and is the last country in the world Washington would want to see destabilised? Is this hypocrisy and how long can it be tolerated?

(4) *Intervention versus non-intervention* As an aggressive human rights policy is pursued, it must be recognised that it entails interfering in the internal affairs of other nations. How can one best reconcile (which the Carter administration failed to do) non-intervention on the one hand, which is generally supported, with human rights advocacy,

which is also supported? How far should one go and how hard can human rights be promoted before the policy becomes counter-productive?

(5) *What instruments?* Suppose quiet diplomacy is not enough to achieve the human rights goals desired. Should public diplomacy then be employed; coercive diplomacy? Sanctions? Military interventions? The issue is not just what are the most effective instruments of policy but also a calculus of how far the US is willing to go to achieve desired goals, and at what costs?

(6) *Balance with other interests.* Human rights and democracy are important US interests, and they have recently become even most important. But they are not the only interests, and in some circum-stances they may not even be the most important – although that discussion is likely to set off the alarm bells of the US domestic debate as El Salvador and South Africa did in the 1980s. Saudi Arabia is the most obvious case: oil takes precedence over human rights considerations. In Peru, the US interest in counter-narcotics may have a higher priority than human rights abuses by the Peruvian military or the abrogation of certain constitutional rights by President Alberto Fujimori. In Mexico the desire for continued stability in a large neighbour takes precedence over democratisation.

(7) *Backsliding.* The US has been euphoric over the transition to democracy in so many countries in recent years that it has paid insufficient attention to the policy responses it should have if democracy is overthrown or reversed. Haiti is the most obvious case, and while Haiti is not typical or representative of Latin America, the debate over US policy there has been deeply divisive. Yet what if democracy were reversed or destroyed in a large and important country: Peru, Venezuela, Colombia, the Philippines, Brazil, or Argentina? What if it is reversed in Poland or Russia? The prospect is so distasteful that contingency plans have not been sufficiently thought through and formulated should democracy be overthrown. What precisely should the US response be? If sanctions do not work, are the American people willing to intervene militarily to restore democracy? What if democracy is reversed not in some isolated, small, and unimportant country but there is a whole *wave* of reversions to authoritarianism as in the 1960s? What could or should the United States do?

(8) *Democratic consolidation.* During the 1980s the US concentrated on *establishing* democracy: creating the conditions for and then holding elections. Yet a genuinely functioning and long-term democracy

requires more than a single election; it requires an institutional infrastructure (political parties, interest groups), a climate of opinion ('civic
political culture') conductive to a workable democracy, and public
policies that enhance and support democracy in the long run. The tasks
of democratic *consolidation* may well be even more demanding, and
certainly imply a far longer commitment than the initial establishment of
democracy. Haiti is a case in point: even if the US succeeds in re-
establishing a democratic government, does anyone believe that in the
absence of any viable institutions or infrastructure in that country that
democratic consolidation – and hence the need for a continued US
presence – will not require a *very* long time and a mammoth commitment of resources? Somalia may be at an even less politically developed
level in these regards than Haiti. Where would the resources in this time
of budget cutbacks, declining foreign aid, military reductions, and
popular impatience with long-term foreign commitments come from? It
must be acknowledged that democracy-building is a very long, hard, and
expensive process.

(9) *Democracy and socio-economic development*. An even harder
question is whether democracy is even suitable and supportable in these
countries. We tread on dangerous ground here because a widespread
assumption of popular opinion is that American know-how and
influence can succeed in democratising even the poorest country. Yet a
wealth of social science literature suggests that, with some exceptions,
democracy is likely to prosper and become consolidated in countries
that have a sufficiently high level of socio-economic development (and
hence a large middle class, etc.) that representative institutions can be
supported and develop firm foundations.[11] Those who would have US
forces rush into Haiti or Somalia, for example; or into other very poor
countries in order to secure democracy should know that would likely
require a *40–50* year occupation at enormous political and financial
costs. Finally, there is a need to focus on the issue of creating versus
preserving democracy. The first implies starting from scratch (again
Haiti or Somalia), creating something out of nothing, building democracy where none had existed before – an almost impossible job. The
second involves supporting an already existing but now troubled and
politically unstable democracy (Peru, Venezuela), bolstering a possibly
fragile democratic regime that is already in place, where the political
culture is already supportive of democracy and where democratic
institutions already function albeit imperfectly. This second task is not
only far easier but it is likely to produce successful foreign policy that

enjoys popular support. The first strategy is far more difficult, less likely to be successful, and Americans lack the skills to implement it.

Now if these complex issues can be resolved – and there are signs that in recent years policy *has* managed to accomplish some of these or at least blur and fudge over the difficulties – one can have a successful human rights/democratisation policy that goes beyond the apple pie and motherhood level. In short, more than rosy incantations in support of democracy and human rights is needed; there also needs to be hard thinking on these tougher and more complicated issues before a successful and long-term policy can produce effective results.

Global Implications

The programmes from the 1960s (even earlier if one goes back to Presidents William McKinley, Theodore Roosevelt, and Woodrow Wilson – or even to James Polk!) in support of democracy and human rights largely grew out of the Latin American experience. The Soviet Union, Eastern Europe, China and the Middle East were thought to be either too volatile for a successful human rights policy, or else too dangerous, or with the stakes too high for other reasons – for example, Soviet missiles or Saudi oil. Latin America, because the stakes and/or costs of a mistake were assumed to be lower, and because it is close to home and subject to American pressures, was the venue where all manner of programmes were experimented with, from agrarian reform and community development in the 1960s, to family planning and human rights in the 1970s, to democratisation in the 1980s. In this sense, Latin America has been a guinea pig, a political and sociological laboratory for all manner of US reform programmes from time immemorial, but mostly from the 1960s.

The successes, mostly unanticipated by foreign policy specialists, of the democracy/human rights programme in Latin America have by now helped elevate this aspect of US policy to a global dimension. The US now has a set of institutions (the National Endowment for Democracy, Republican and Democratic international institutes) for the spread of democracy, a democracy office in the Agency for International Development, a democracy/human rights bureau at the State Department, a variety of agencies for observing elections, and a host of special interest groups to help support the cause) to further the democracy/human rights agenda. President Clinton and Secretary of State Christopher now proclaim – and no longer just rhetorically – that the promotion of democracy abroad is at the heart of their foreign policy. Democracy has become *the* central unifying theme of the diverse foreign affairs bureaucracies. When one asks what now is US policy in Russia, the former Soviet republics, Eastern Europe, Cambodia, Vietnam, Africa, and the Middle East – to say nothing of Latin America – the answer invariably is *democracy*.

This emphasis has received added impetus because of the end of the Cold War. The cessation of the Cold War not only terminated the superpower competition between the United States and the USSR but it also led to the fall of the Berlin Wall and the unification of Germany, the freedom and democratisation of Eastern Europe, the breakup of the Soviet Union, and the easing and negotiations for the ending of various regional conflicts: in Cambodia, Southern Africa, the Horn of Africa, and Central America. Not only did these momentous international events flow from the withering or atrophying of the Cold War but the Cold War's end also stimulated immense domestic changes in the countries with which the US has long been concerned. Among other things it has led to the declining popularity of communist parties worldwide, the decline of various guerrillas movements, the discrediting of the left in various countries, and the bankruptcy of such regimes as Castro's Cuba as models of Third World development.

All these changes have made the democracy/human rights agenda even more attractive than before. We can now afford to talk about human rights in countries like China that during the Cold War was considered too sensitive and because other, more important stakes were concerned. During the 45 years of the Cold War, security issues could be used to override all other concerns, but that is no longer the case. In a sense, many 'idealistic' agenda items like democracy and human rights have flourished only in times of peace, as luxuries, not in times of crisis or war – even Cold War. But now there is that peace; there is that luxury. So it can be expected that human rights/democracy issues will achieve even greater importance than before and on a global scale. President Carter was premature in elevating human rights to *the* central position in his foreign policy before the Cold War had ended; but now that it *has* ended one can anticipate to see far greater democracy/human rights emphasis.

This emphasis on democracy and human rights is not without its problems, however. First, although there has been progress in some areas, the ten dilemmas discussed in the preceding section have by no means been resolved – or even addressed in some areas. Second, the policy may still be selective in some cases: witness the dispute in the Bush administration over applying human rights criteria in China, the question of how far (if at all) Washington should push Kuwait or Saudi

Arabia on democracy/human rights issues, or the longtime dispute, whose dimensions are also changing rapidly in the wake of the Cold War, over how hard the US should push Israel to implement Palestinian rights. Third, what of countries like Russia and others where Washington has put so many of its foreign policy eggs in the democracy/free market basket, but where the culture, society and political system seem unsupportive of democracy at least in the short term? Finally, and as hinted at above, one may strongly disagree – as in the case of Haiti – over the situation of human rights in that county, over its causes, and over what should be done about it. Thus, although there is widespread bipartisan consensus on human rights policy, and though the policy now claims universal applicability, there may still be sharp disagreements over the precise human rights situation in a given country, what the United States should do about it, and what should be the trade-off between human rights and other issues of importance in US foreign policy.

DoD and Human Rights Policy

The Department of Defense (DoD) is not an initiator of foreign policy in most instances. Rather its role is to carry out policy decided elsewhere: by the president, the National Security Council, the Department of State, or other agencies. As with the drug war, DoD is charged with implementing policy, not formulating it. Of course in the process of implementation, a great deal of bending, hauling, and modifying may take place. Yet essentially, the Pentagon is given an objective or a mission and instructed to devise plans to carry it out. Therefore, we cannot fault DoD in most cases when the human rights/democratisation programme goes astray. The Pentagon is usually in the circumstances where the policy was designed elsewhere; as with the drug war again, if the policy is faulty or mis-conceptualised, it is the 'elsewhere's' fault, not the military's. As former Secretary of Defense Richard B. Cheney stated, DoD's role is to 'translate foreign policy objectives into operational tasks for the US military'.[12]

The armed forces have been handed the democracy/human rights agenda and instructed to help implement it. DoD does this willingly, even enthusiastically, because democracy is a value that all Americans share. Initially, once more as with drugs, there was some Pentagon resistance to this emphasis because it is not necessarily in accord with the military's primary mission which is to fight and to serve as an armed deterrent. Yet in the aftermath of the Cold War, the democracy/human rights agenda, along with the drug one, was seen as a way of providing the armed focus with a new mission to help justify its budget, personnel, and role. Human rights and democracy call for the US military to act in support of broader US policy goals in this area. In addition, with the broader conception of security that now (which includes counter-narcotics, humanitarian aid, border patrol, nonproliferation, peace-keeping, some level of law enforcement, and other of the so-called 'new agenda' items), the defence of democracy and human rights can also be considered as a security concern.

What then should the military do in this area? In the absence presently of any one, single, overriding objective such as containment of the Soviet Union, DoD will now have a variety, or menu, of roles and objectives. The overall goals of US policy in Latin America continue to be:[13]

(1) Support of democracy and human rights.
(2) Economic development and free economies coupled with equity.
(3) Political stability and the resolution of conflicts through negotiations.
(4) Policies and practices that help preserve the environment.
(5) A strong counter-narcotics policy.
(6) Effective international cooperation to deal with the post-Cold War agenda of arms control, nuclear nonproliferation, and regional security.

We will here focus on the first item, democracy and human rights, and not on the last five of these – except to say that success in the drug war, in achieving economic development or in these other policy areas can also be seen as helping the overall goal of securing democracy and human rights. Recall that the concept of 'security' has recently been broadened to encompass these areas, as well as including the earlier, narrower military definition. But let us confine ourselves now to the democracy/human rights item and ask what the US military can do in this area. Three major areas may be identified: developing civilian understanding of and competence in military affairs, facilitating civil-military dialogue, and encouraging professional competence and ethical standards within the Latin American militaries. Let us look specifically at what should be tackled within these three categories:

(1) Developing civilian understanding and competence in military affairs:

- Include civilians in Expanded International Military Education and Training (EIMET)- and IMET-funded programmes for professional military education.

- Encourage Latin American militaries to include civilians in their advanced security studies schools; encourage civilians to design courses to bring military officers into civilian (such as foreign service) training programmes.
- Require that military assistance programmes be subject to the oversight of US and Latin American civilian officials.
- Develop crisis-action simulations for joint civilian and military participants tailored to the special requirements of different Latin American security establishments.
- Help educate Latin American leaders that while the military should not interfere in civilian affairs, neither should civilians interfere for political purposes in professional military affairs.

(2) Facilitating the civil-military dialogue:

- Increase use of existing DoD, USIA, and other programmes, public and private, to have Latin American officials visit the United States in mixed civilian-military delegations.
- Provide courses and programmes for mixed groups of military and civilian officials at US professional schools.
- Offer to provide more US instructors at Latin American service schools (including military academies) beyond current levels of reciprocal exchange programs; increasingly use DoD civilians as well as military in such programmes.
- Encourage social, cultural, and exchange programmes at all levels that bring together civilian and military elites – meanwhile realistically keeping in mind the social, political, and even racial differences that often separate these groups.

(3) Encouraging professional competence and ethical standards within the Latin American militaries:

- Engage with Latin American military institutions in redefining post-Cold War goals and missions. Encourage a 'capabilities' approach as opposed to a 'threat' approach. Explain how DoD is also wrestling with this new environment.
- Emphasise the interconnectedness of democracy, stability, and free, open markets. Democracy helps solve problems of under-development and instability and is now the only acceptable alternative on a global basis. Without democracy there is only ostracism, pariah status, a cutoff of global aid and loans, and a dismal future for the country and its armed forces.
- Cross-fertilise with service Judge Advocate General offices in

countries that are beginning to examine their own military justice systems and reforming their legal systems.

- Ensure that Latin American military visitors have contact with appropriate DoD civilians.
- Work with the Latin American militaries to develop competence in newer non-fighting pursuits: peacekeeping (as in Argentina), nonproliferation, civic action/nation-building, as well as counter-narcotics. Channel the Latin American military into constructive pursuits that help enhance its self-esteem and professionalism while avoiding political activities.
- Assist the Latin American countries in rebuilding the inter-American security system. Help reconstruct the Inter-American Defense Board as well as the Organization of American States. Expand contacts and interchange aimed at establishing inter-American defence arrangements parallel and complementary to the new inter-American trade agreements. Explore also an associated status in NATO for Latin American countries.
- Be prepared in emergency situations when democracy is severely threatened (as in Venezuela) for extraordinary efforts. These may include, on a short-term basis to get through the emergency, exhorting military officers to help preserve constitutional government, or even supplementing woefully inadequate basic military salaries.
- In general, work *with* the Latin American military institutions, which are presently severely threatened and subject to reprisals in some countries for past authoritarian practices, rather than against them. Be prepared to listen with empathy and to understand the situation of Latin American military officers, whose political culture and institutional responsibilities are often different from those in the US, rather than from the point of view of superiority or knee-jerk condemnation.

Conclusions

Since the 1960s the promotion of human rights and democracy has become on integral part of United States foreign policy. The policy is now far more realistic and pragmatic than it was when earlier proposed; the human rights policy has helped resolve the long dispute between idealism and realism in foreign policy and has made many significant contributions to American successes in recent years – not the least being the fall of the Soviet Union whose legitimacy was in part undermined by human rights considerations. The policy enjoys bipartisan and near-universal consensus; there is no longer any dissent from it

Human rights is now seen as part of a broader strategy of promoting democracy and economic growth through free markets. Free political systems and free economies – that is what America stands for. Human rights and democratisation serve *concrete* American *interests*. The institutional machinery in support of democracy and human rights has now grown up, and the United States is now far more sophisticated and successful in the implementation of the policy than in earlier years. By this time human rights/democratisation has emerged from its earlier regional focus (Latin America primarily) to become a truly global concern.

The end of the Cold War gives even greater importance to the democracy/human rights agenda. With the historic enemy, the Soviet Union, now in tatters, and with no future competing superpower in sight (some other countries may have economic power but they do not have the combination of political, economic, diplomatic, and military power that the United States has), human rights and democratisation are certain to achieve even greater significance than in the past. In non-war, non-crisis, non-threatening situations as at present such 'new agenda' items as human rights and democratisation emerge at the forefront of foreign policy concerns.

There remain, however, many unresolved issues in implementing an effective human rights/democracy policy. Policy-makers, including military officials, need to understand these harder issues, which are at the heart of a rights/democracy policy. Policy-makers also need to comprehend the different, often culturally-based interpretations, meanings and priorities of human rights in different societies, while also holding fast to an emerging legal and political consensus on global standards of human rights/democratisation. On this more enlightened, realistic basis, a strong human rights/democracy policy can go forward on a foundation that is not only morally correct but also serves American interests. The United States armed forces can and will have significant roles to play in the implementation of this policy.

NOTES

1. Walter LaFeber, *Liberty and Power; US Diplomatic History, 1750–1943* (Washington, DC: American Historical Assoc., 1991).
2. The quote has been attributed to John Foster Dulles.
3. A careful, balanced treatment is Larman C. Wilson, 'Human Rights in United States Foreign Policy', in Don Piper and Ronald Terchek (eds.), *Interaction: Foreign Policy and Public Policy* (Washington, DC: American Enterprise Inst. for Public Policy Res., 1983), pp.178–208.

4. See my assessment in Howard J. Wiarda, *The Democratic Revolution in Latin America* (NY: A Twentieth Century Fund Book, Holmes and Meier, 1990).
5. Anthony Lake, *Somoza Falling* (Boston: Houghton-Mifflin, 1989).
6. Robert E. Osgood, 'The Carter Policy in Perspective', *SAIS Review* I (Winter 1981), pp.11–22; Terry L. Deibel, 'Jimmy Carter, Denial of Power and the Quest for Values', Ch.3 in *Presidents, Public Opinion, and Power* (NY: Foreign Policy Assoc., 1987); and Stanley Hoffman, 'Requiem', *Foreign Policy* 42 (Spring 1981), pp.3–26.
7. Daniel Pipes and Adam Garfinkle (eds.), *Friendly Tyrants: An American Dilemma* (NY: St Martin's Press, 1991).
8. See Howard J. Wiarda, *Human Rights and US Human Rights Policy* (Washington, DC: American Enterprise Inst. for Public Policy Res., 1982).
9. Tamar Jacoby, 'The Reagan Turnaround on Human Rights', *Foreign Affairs* (Summer 1986), pp.1066–86.
10. A full examination is in Wiarda, *Democratic Revolution* (note 4).
11. Seymour Martin Lipset, *Political Man* (Garden City, NY: Doubleday, 1960); W.W. Rostow, *The Stages of Economic Growth* (Cambridge, UK: CUP 1960); Larry Diamond *et. al*, *Democracy in Developing Countries*, 4 vols. (Boulder, CO: Lynne Rienner, 1980s).
12. Richard B. Cheney, *Annual Report to the President and Congress* (Washington, DC: Dept. of Defense, Feb. 1992), p.13.
13. The materials in this section derive from a report of the Institute for National Strategic Studies (INSS), 'DOD Planning for the Americas', Washington, DC, 4 Jan. 1993. The author helped participate in the preparation of this report but has added his own points and emphases in the present paper. See also L. Erik Kjonnerod (ed.), *Evolving US Strategy for Latin America and the Caribbean* (Washington, DC: National Defense UP, 1992).

Military Engineers: Nation Assistance in the New World Order

JACK A. LECUYER

This paper will discuss the role of the US Military Engineers – Army, Navy, Marines and Air Force – and the concept of Nation Development and its role in the emerging deter-stability-win equation of national security. My hands-on experience in this area in Latin America is somewhat dated, but my vantage point from a policy perspective in Washington might be useful. My two great efforts while I was assigned to US Southern Command (USSOUTHCOM) were to advocate that we discard the term 'Nation Building' because of its baggage and instead substitute the phrase 'Nation Development' and to urge acceptance of the notion that joint, combined and interagency Nation Development campaign plans could and should be developed. In my view Nation Development is a strategic imperative for the achievement of United States security interests in Latin America . . . and I suggest that the events of the post-Cold War era simply reinforce that belief. As we move from a strategy of containment to one of collective engagement, the instrumentalities for achieving these US national security interests are both more sophisticated and inter-related than at any time in the past. A strategy of peacetime engagement, forward presence, and crisis response to protect American interests will be more difficult to implement than in the Cold War years.

Today, the United States has an opportunity to address the full range of concepts embodied in the term national security. It has become increasingly clear that national security is a pluralistic or multifaceted concept, and that it extends beyond military security in a narrow sense. For example, concerns about the health of the economy, competitiveness, and trade deficits have been added to the security agenda. Similarly, American international interests are best served by democratic values, institutions, and free market economies. The promotion of such an environment is no longer challenged as a security issue. A sense of national prosperity is now viewed as the underlying condition for national security. What is sometimes challenged is the role military forces and their supporting agencies can and should play in national security strategy. As direct military threats to the physical survival of the United States are reduced, greater attention and resources can be applied to other issues. National security will increasingly mean more than preserving the integrity of American society; it will mean preserving and enhancing the quality of life.

These circumstances, taken together, require the United States to meet a different set of challenges in pursuit of national security. Perhaps the most obvious of these challenges is instability in emerging nations which remain central to US national security interests. First, the economic health of the United States is increasingly tied to the developing world. Raw materials and agricultural produce from these nations will remain important to the American market. Economic growth will increase the already substantial demand for American products in the developing nations. Yet the issue of debt – both government to government loans and commercial credit – overshadows economic relationships with many developing nations.

Second, despite the disappearance of direct conflict and competition between the US and the former Soviet Union, the relationship with Russia and the other nuclear powers in the world will remain competitive.

Finally, at least two factors affecting the quality of life in the United States originate in the poverty and low standard of living found in the developing nations. The consumption of illegal drugs and illegal immigration are having an increasingly adverse effect on American society. The United States must take steps to reduce demand for drugs while assisting nations seeking to eliminate their production. In addition, recent years have seen some 1,000,000 immigrants – legal and illegal – enter the United States annually. Many were fleeing violence and economic deprivation in their native lands in Central America.

Let me now turn to a deter-stability-win equation to indicate how the Military Engineers, to include the Army and Headquarters, US Army Corps of Engineers, can be very real players in achieving America's strategic objectives in Latin America.

The principal purpose of armed forces is both to deter and win a nation's wars. The armed forces look at the world through operational lenses. Over the past five years, senior army leaders have articulated the notion of the Army as a relevant strategic force. A parallel development has been the replacement of the traditional notion of the spectrum of conflict with the concept of an operational continuum. This concept of an operational continuum presents us with a much more realistic assessment of how to deal with operational challenges to national security, and suggests that there are several threats affecting national security and prosperity which must be dealt with before sending combat forces into a conflict situation.

FIGURE 1

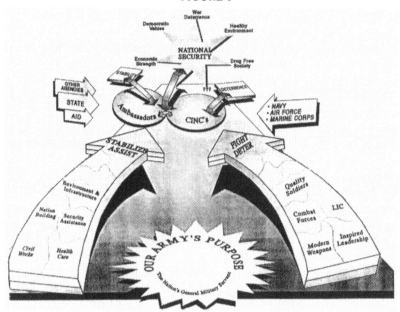

FIGURE 2

THE OPERATIONAL CONTINUUM

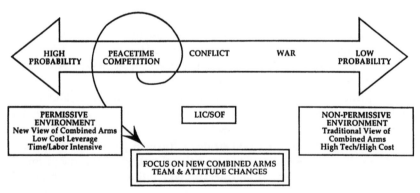

* Enable Military to Serve Multiple Roles
  - Deterrence
    - Defense
      - Stability/Security
      - Development

* Principles of War Still Apply ——▶ Project Power to Point of Influence
* Joint/Service Doctrine to be Written

While he was CINCSOUTH, General Fred F. Woerner, developed the notion of High Probability Conflict (HPC) to describe the peacetime competition that takes place in developing nations. Both General Woerner and the Army understood the need to focus on a new combined arms team and institutional attitude changes required of the military and government agencies forward deployed in areas of Latin America. If one thinks of an operational continuum, then one can certainly describe the environments in which military forces and the Army could be operationally employed to the benefit of a host nation. Accordingly, we need to examine how the military – all services – can serve multiple roles in the achievement of national strategic objectives. Even in peacetime engagement, the principles of war will still apply because then the elements of national power, including, but not limited to, military forces are being projected to the point of influence. In the traditional sense, this equates with the principle of mass. Fortunately, the joint and service doctrine which would institutionalise this notion of the operational continuum was published in June 1993.

Earlier, I suggested that stability was the underpinning of national security in the Deter-Stability-Win equation. I have given some thought as to a model which shows the relationship of national security to the concept of nation development. If we approach the model (Figure 3), and view the columns, which support this remarkable edifice called national security, I think it is possible to take the policy objectives first enunciated by President Ronald Reagan in 1981, reaffirmed in the 1988 publication of Discriminate Deterrence, and at least tacitly accepted by the Bush administration as the pillars which undergird the notion of stability. President-Elect Clinton's own sense of a vibrant global economy as the precondition to America's own national prosperity only reinforces this notion.

I would simply modify the Reagan notion of defence against global communism to that of defence of our vital national interests . . . many of them economic or resource based.

Thus, I have shown defence of national vital interests, diplomacy, development and democratisation as those elements which contribute to the stability equation. If global and regional stability are the preconditions for national security, then it becomes clear how nation development fits into this equation. The various nation development activities shown in the steps to this building are the foundations of stability. Military Engineers – to include the Army Corps of Engineers – have a role to play in this overall strategic effort.

Over the past 20 years, each CINCSOUTH has argued that sustaining US national security interests in Latin America is not so much a function of traditional military operations but rather, a function of regional

FIGURE 3

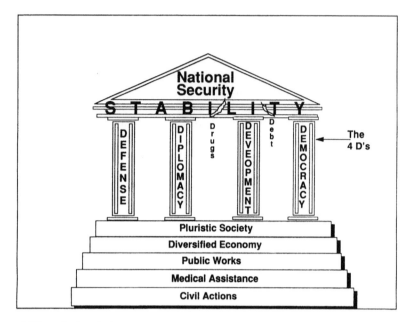

stability. Indeed, if one thinks of how Washington should defend its national interests in the Panama Canal Zone, it is not at all clear that the use of US troops deployed in a traditional military role would, in fact, guarantee the integrity of the Canal. A far more persuasive argument would suggest that the best defence of the canal and vital US interests is regional stability based on regional commitment to democratic institutions and economic development.

With this in mind, it is useful to review the range of threats to stability in Latin America outlined earlier. Such threats include the extreme burdens of national debt, drugs and vast population migrations. These problems are compounded by an enduring lack of infrastructure, coupled with traditional military or paramilitary threats posed by insurgent or narco-trafficking groups, which make domestic security difficult in several of the 17 nations.

Finally, there is a series of outside threats which deal with environmental concerns and natural disasters. These threats and the competition for scarce resources suggest that any strategy for Latin America which focuses on stability as its strategic objective must be a strategy based on tailored force options that involve integration of all the instruments of national power – diplomatic, economic, and military. In military terms, Latin America is best seen as an economy of force theatre.

FIGURE 4

Many have tried to understand stability. General John R. Galvin perhaps expressed the relationship best when he suggested that stability is really a function of the triangular relationship between the government, the people and that range of threats already discussed. Those threats could be either an insurgent or the narco-trafficante group or perhaps terrorists. In this fragile relationship, the government must do three things:

- It must defeat or convert those groups which pose a threat to democratic institutions;
- It must protect the people from those threats in order to stabilise the democratic processes, and most important;
- It must also promote indigenous institutions which permit pluralistic society and economic development.

Thus, the challenge for US policy is how to take enduring semi-autonomous host nation institutions such as the army or civilian ministries traditionally run as hotbeds of nepotism and use them as stable agents for change and legitimate forces within democratic society. Like America's Army, the Latin American military must be seen as legitimate agents of social change. Such military forces, always focused on providing a security and economic shield for the people they serve and subordinate to civil control, can promote social stability for an increasingly democratic Latin American society.

Legitimate nation development must be defined in the broadest context possible for the host nation culture and not necessarily in terms of US concepts. We should focus on the function rather than the equivalent US government agency . . . for example, viewing law enforcement as strictly a function of the 'police' may or may not correspond to realities in Latin American nations where the Army has traditionally performed that function.

In Latin America, the US long-term security objectives should not be held hostage to short-term political objectives. Nation development was and perhaps still is an implied rather than specified task, but is burdened by the legacy of past failures of short-sighted policies. Yet I believe that nation development can be an achievable objective over time – indeed it is probably the best definition of what is beginning to be called peacemaking. My purpose is to suggest to you some engineer tools and instrumentalities that would help attack these problems in dealing with long-term efforts to ensure stability while still permitting achievement of the more highly visible short-term political objectives and operational military objectives.

First, let it be understood that stability does not mean 'status quo'. Rather, change is the 'norm'. In Latin America the problem with change is not that it takes place, but rather, that it takes place with differential rates of change in the various spheres of social, economic, political, and military life – within each and every country and region.

If we understand that change is the norm, then it is probably best to define stability in terms of change. In that regard, I would suggest that stability requires that change takes place in an orderly and coordinated fashion, and should be compatible with US interests – democratic and economic development – and in accordance with the norms of international law. If change is the norm, then proper nation development requires long-term US commitments to ensure national stability.

Achieving consensus for a long-haul, national commitment to nation development abroad when the US has so many problems at home is no mean task. It is useful to look at some of the reasons why there may not be a national constituency for such an undertaking by the military forces. Those constraints include:

- US public opinion and short-term horizons for success
- Absorption capacity over time of Host Nation/Region

    and Country Teams
 – Development of coherent and consistent implementing func-
    tional strategies
 – Time lines for resource availability
 – Tradeoffs in regions/country/theatre
 – Inter-theatre and intra-theatre competition for resources
 – Sanctions against foreign military supplies
 – Lack of national concepts of leverage/notions of a payoff matrix
    to achieve multiple objectives

Each of the constraints – whether it be short-time horizons for
political success or the absorption capacity of a nation over time, or
interagency and inter-theatre competition – contributes to a 'national'
and agency mental block for the acceptance of an integrated strategy of
nation development as an explicit mission in the operational continuum.
For example, in examining the drug problem today in Latin America,
one finds that in many cases the US can contribute substantially to
nation development and the development of alternative crops through
the provision of engineer equipment from foreign supply sources to be
used by host nation armies to construct national infrastructure. However, the sanctions imposed on the Andean Ridge countries for failure
to confront drug problems, debt reduction, and human rights pose
insurmountable barriers to attacking these problems. Moreover,
because of the way host nation government agencies are currently
arrayed, the concept of leverage and the notion of a payoff matrix to
achieve multiple directives simply is not part of the political calculus.
    The constraints outlined are not exhaustive; however, they result in a
gap in American ability to face squarely the notion of nation development as a strategic imperative.
    The model shown here in Figure 5 simply suggests that if one regards
development as an underlying concept which leads to stability, there is a
gap in US ability to contribute more fully to the achievement of its
strategic goal. As the model indicates, there are ongoing activities which
can create the necessary conditions for development. However, the
many constraints which I listed result in US inability to fully employ an
economy of force strategy to achieve nation development in Latin
American countries.
    This model demonstrates first of all the limited absorption capacity of
host nations to accept foreign assistance. Moreover it suggests that these
are disconnects with the US federal government arising from inter/intra
agency competition, local interpretation of US policy, and the location

FIGURE 5

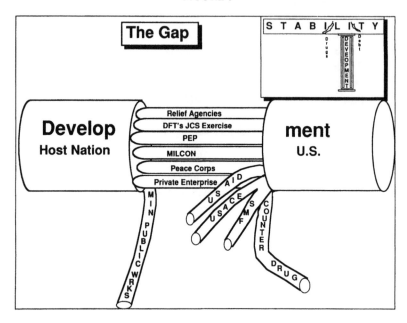

of management in one 'stovepipe' and funding in a variety of other stovepipes. Finally, there is the problem of the traditional disconnect at the functional interface which is based on Washington's perception of the world and where legitimate roles of government lie rather than the governmental organisation of the host nation. As an example, often the policy responsibilities for public infrastructure and public works in Latin American countries are located in one or more civilian ministries; however, as in the case of Peru, the military may be charged with a primary role of execution in nation development. Similarly, on the country team, the real public works expertise may often reside not with the civilian agency holders of resources but with the military engineers, to include HQ USACE. The disconnect comes when those in charge of country strategies argue that US Military Engineers in uniform cannot and should not contaminate traditional assistance programs (e.g., Agency for International Development) or interface with host nation civilian ministries more effectively to prosecute the concept of nation development and promote the legitimate role for military forces in a developing and democratic society.

   With this in mind, let me suggest how the engineer portion of strategy for nation development might be applied to USSOUTHCOM and Latin America.

There is ample evidence that Commanders-in-chief from General Paul Gorman through General George Joulwan have spent a considerable amount of time defining the regional security objectives in terms of a SOUTHCOM Mission Essential Task List (METL). There are apparently over 450 different taskings in some 50 Joint Chiefs of Staff (JCS)/ Department of Defence (DoD) documents which affect SOUTHCOM. Many of these are overlapping and SOUTHCOM has at least been able to distill those taskings down into a METL. As one reviews these lists, however, one can only come to the conclusion that while nation development is an implied task, nowhere has SOUTHCOM been given the specific and explicit objective for nation development by the JCS. It is not a METL task. Nor is it an explicit objective of the Country Teams.

In addition to analysing US objectives and security objectives in SOUTHCOM, the current regional strategy documents also suggest that several resource inventories have been conducted to integrate all the elements of national power in a regional economic strategy. These inventories include budgetary programmes such as foreign military supply, JCS exercises, interagency joint and combined counter-drug operations and Title 10 MCA (exercise related construction) as well as functional areas such as medicine, engineering, etc. In short, despite the lack of formal national policy guidance, there are evolving implementing functional strategies currently in place – to include engineers – which if effectively integrated and formally structured and resourced over a five-to-ten-year period could contribute to achievement of US national security objectives in Latin America.

Figure 6 shows the resource inventory of traditional Military Engineer tools that exists for the implementation of an Engineer portion of the strategy to support nation development.

These basic tools with a diverse set of embedded capabilities, have all been employed in the past in some form to support the Country Teams.

As an example of how these tools have been used to implement an engineer nation development strategy, I offer the example of Guatemala – a country where until 1988, the Country Team – strongly influenced by their concerns about the military engineers' 'hyperactivity' in Honduras – stubbornly resisted the notion that military forces could play an important role in the operational continuum to achieve national security objectives through nation development and stability. Figure 7 shows an organic Engineer strategy developed to support both CINC-SOUTH and Ambassador Michel. It was based on the absorption and sustainment capabilities of the Country Team, and shows a gradual ramping up of the effort, consistent with the efforts and capabilities of the highly qualified Guatemalan Army Engineers and their own civilian

FIGURE 6

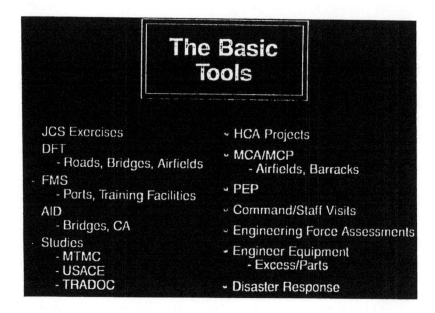

The Basic Tools

JCS Exercises	⌄ HCA Projects
DFT	⌄ MCA/MCP
- Roads, Bridges, Airfields	- Airfields, Barracks
⌄ FMS	⌄ PEP
- Ports, Training Facilities	
AID	⌄ Command/Staff Visits
- Bridges, CA	⌄ Engineering Force Assessments
⌄ Studies	⌄ Engineer Equipment
- MTMC	- Excess/Parts
- USACE	
- TRADOC	⌄ Disaster Response

Ministry of Public Works. The results that the Guatemalan engineers are achieving today are nothing short of phenomenal considering the adverse conditions and terrain, the insurgency and intractable narcotrafficking activity, and the condition of their construction equipment. There is a local saying that captures the essence of what military engineers can do to enhance stability in a nation emerging from the 40-year long sleep and support for a authoritarian military government as the counter to communist expansion. That saying is, 'Where the road ends, the insurgency begins.' A joint Army-Caterpillar effort to direct nearly $1 million of foreign military supply to repair parts for aging engineer equipment was a key catalyst for change in the US Army approach from one of denial to one of full military cooperation and participation with the Country Team.

In Fiscal Year 1993 US and Guatemalan military engineers will conduct Exercise 'Fuertes Caminos' to build additional roads and other vitally needed infrastructure.

This strategy could be leveraged even further if the total resources available to USACE and other US government agencies were made part of the overall equation for nation development. USACE resources applied in various areas could reinforce both the C-in-C and a country ambassador ensuring a successful implementation of a leveraged econ-

FIGURE 7

POTENTIAL TOOLS BASED
ON TOTAL USACE CAPABILITY
FOR NATION BUILDING

- **CIVIL WORKS SUPPORT FOR AMBASSADOR/CINC**

  - Agent of Choice for all studies, design and construction for capital investment
  - Provide Engineer "Staff Offices" to MILGP/SCEN Regional Desk
  - Management Tools/Techniques
    - Project Planning (absorption capability/MOE-B/C measures)
    - Life Cycle Project Management
    - Cost Sharing/Funds Accountability
    - Partnering
  - Environmental Protection/Enhancement
    - HTW
    - Superfund
    - 404 (b) Permits

- **JOINT VENTURE FUNDING**

  - Leverage
  - Non-DOD Funding Sources (AID, ESF, Private Sector)
  - Multinational Funding

- **POLITICAL LEVERAGE**

  - ASA (CW) Relationship with DOS/DOE/Congress
  - COE Relationship with Army/AF as Construcion Agent
  - COE Relationship with Congress through MILCON/CW
  - COE Relationship with Others Overseas

- **PEOPLE/RESOURCES**

  - Redirect/Expand PEP and LATAM Coop
  - Expand AERB and Language Training
  - DAC in Host Nation Ministry ("PEP")

- **TECHNOLOGY TRANSFER**

  - USACE Labs
  - Standardized Design Packages (to TO Standards)
  - State of Art
  - Reverse CPAR

- **COUNTERDRUG EFFORT**

  - Bridge to Alternatives for Coca Productions
  - Economic Infrastructure
  - Drainage
  - Water Supply
  - Ground Water Study
  - Hydroelectric

- **DISASTER PREPAREDNESS**

  - Earthquake
  - HTW
  - Floodplain Mapping
  - Dam Safety

FIGURE 8

Country Example: Guatemala

FY 88: SCEN Staff Visits
   Engineer Equipment and Force Structure Assessment
   MTT: Mine/Countermine
   Exchange Visits

FY 89: SCEN Staff Visits
   FMS: Engineer Repar Parts
   DFT - Lake Atitlan - Rock Drilling/Blasting
   Excess Engineer Equipment Procurement
   COE Visit
   Airfield Pavement Evaluation
   Visit of GT Engineers to SOUTHCOM and Honduras

FY 90: Army and Navy DFTs
   Continue Excess Equipment Initiative
   SCEN Visits
   Repairs to Airfield Parking Apron

FY 91: Expanded DFT Program
   Formalized PEP
   Command and Staff Visits

omy of force strategy for nation development. Many have already been used in Latin America, often paid for with C-in-C initiative or study funds. Some of these capabilities are simply listed here and it is suggested that each of them could be applied to overcome the implementation gap indicated earlier.

Obviously this is not a exhaustive list, but it does indicate the kinds of capabilities that the Army Corps of Engineers could bring to bear in Latin America. It would be remiss of me if I did not acknowledge the many services already supplied by the Corps – services which have ranged from subject matter expert exchanges on roller compacted concrete and earthquake construction with Brazil to extensive infrastructure construction in Honduras and El Salvador to disaster relief in Ecuador, Costa Rica, and El Salvador. Yet military engineers and the Corps of Engineers are not always miracle makers. For example, with regard to the national counter-drug effort, they cannot provide alternate crops. However, Military Engineers – uniformed and the Corps – can provide the infrastructure which provides the basis for alternative crops and the transportation of those crops to market. The 'Fuertes Caminos'/ 'Ponte de la Paz' exercises in Honduras, Panama, Ecuador, Bolivia, and Costa Rica and numerous small projects throughout Latin America ranging from bridges in Belize, airfields in Bolivia, well drilling and port construction in Honduras, to repair of a hospital electrical system in

Bolivia and disaster relief in Panama, El Salvador, Costa Rica, Ecuador and Peru are but several examples of this.

Thus, the gap in nation development described earlier could be overcome if it is understood that the most important interface is not the single agency-to-agency interface, but rather, the functional management interface between the limited financial and management resources which could be made available through the United States and the governmental structure of the recipient host nation.

In short, there is a need to find a better way to pair US Military Engineer capabilities and USACE management and contracting capabilities with USAID, foreign military supply, and counter-drug fund, to facilitate public works as part of the country team's nation development strategy.

Most exciting is the thought that you can do nation development in the Andean Ridge in a situation of undeclared war – to attack General Joulwan's Beehive – and still fight the war on drugs.

I have tried to portray the development of an implementing Engineer functional strategy for the concept of nation development in the coca leaf-producing countries of Peru, Ecuador and Bolivia. These strategies are not unlike earlier strategies in Honduras and El Salvador – only now the US seeks to contain illegal drugs at the source rather than preventing the spread of global communism. The strategies reflect only the application of traditional military engineer tools, with the concurrence of the Ambassador and the Country Team. I would simply reaffirm that point made earlier – that in the case of Peru, application of even traditional strategies could be enhanced substantially if we could find a way to lift legislated foreign military supply sanctions for the purchase or transfer of excess DoD engineer equipment and parts or apply some of the counter-drug funding to that effort.

In each of the Andean Ridge countries, the host nation military engineers have traditionally played a significant role in national development. In Peru, the Army is specifically tasked under Article 208 of the Constitution to provide for nation development, and has the force structure (some 19 battalions), to do so. Joint training, and exercises with US Military Engineers along with the capabilities of the Corps of Engineers to improve the situation for nation development could contribute to the economic stability and change so necessary to counter the drug threat and restore economic viability to these nations.

The bottom line is quite simply this – as America moves to a national grand strategy of collective engagement, there must be a plan to bridge the current institutional gaps in implementing a nation development strategy. Understanding that the Ambassador has the lead, we need to

find a way to task organise both the Country Team and all of those
military engineer resources available through the C-in-C to support host
nation civilian ministries. There is a synergistic effect for nation
development which can be applied through the integration of all
available US resources – be they management or funding – for nation
development. Obviously there are some limitations to what can or
should be done. Funding is always a first order problem . . . and the
notion of venture capital pooling and enhancing increasingly scarce
federal resources is a paramount priority. Beyond funding limitations
the effort must be *designed to succeed over time* and some measures of
effectiveness and benefit/cost ratios must be developed for judging how
and when these scarce resources will be applied (Figure 9).

FIGURE 9

THINKING OF NATION DEVELOPMENT IN TERMS OF TIME

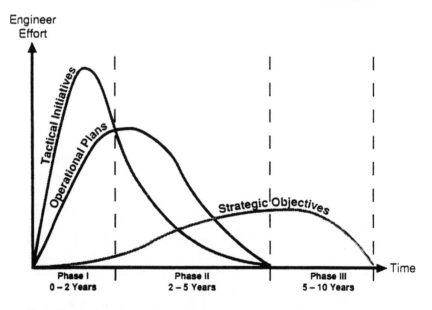

Equally important, we must assiduously avoid the traditional problem
of raising expectations through visits and promises only to leave host
nations with dashed hopes as resources are not made available or when
the visitors fail to complete a project or exercise to standard. And
finally, as is true with all change, a way must be found to develop
indigenous institutions and capabilities which promote host nation
ownership of the concept of nation development. Equally important
partnership must be constantly promoted between all US military

forces, Latin American armies, US government agencies, and host nation civilian ministries to achieve the strategic imperative of nation development.

Strategies are more than rhetoric and logic. They are prescriptions for the commitment of resources. In the case of nation development, the resources range from people – the right kind of people in the right kind of places – to institutions such as the Military Engineers and the Army Corps of Engineers – to a very extensive list of player agencies, and limited sources of dollars. The budgetary and programme support for nation development in Latin America constitutes less than one-half of one per cent of the DoD budget. The funds are in small programme of $10 to $20 million and located in several agencies. Yet each of these programmes can be brought to bear, hopefully in conjunction with one another, as well as funding available from other US agencies – AID, US Development Agency, FDO, Drug Enforcement Agency, etc. – to work on the situation for maximum effect. The key to achieving this objective is the notion of developing the political support, not only within DoD, but also in that external environment which includes other government agencies such as the State Department, the administration, Congress, the American public, the country team, and the host nation.

To consider the notion of public support at a time when America's economy is troubled by huge federal and local government deficits, there are probably four major categories of audiences which need to be addressed. The problem of political support is twofold and resolution requires a deliberate strategy, which some have called the war of information. Communication links must be established between the national command authority, the forward-deployed C-in-C, the Country Team and the host nation and to overcome the tremendous communications and understanding problems that exist within each of those agencies. The information campaign to achieve a national consensus for a strategic use of Military Engineers in operational deployments for nation development is increasingly urgent, witness the national commitment of military forces in providing comfort to Somalia and other troubled areas of the world. These strategies must be designed to overcome both the breakage in the lines of communication and authority between agencies and the problems within the agencies. This campaign requires explicit consideration of objectives, target audiences, identification of messages for those audiences, and exploitation of opportunities to achieve unanimity of thought in this tremendous effort.

The bottom line is quite simple. Regional and local stability is the essential element which undergirds the US national security effort in Latin America. However, in all of the tasking documents, be they

Department of State or Department of Defense, nation development is at most an implied task. Specifically designed military forces do not and should not accomplish only these tasks; these capabilities are embedded in US combat forces and can be accomplished through operational deployments. Yet, it must be insisted that operational use of these forces clearly accomplishes US unit training objectives . . . by training to standard and leaving a properly completed project or initiative behind. Equally important, these deployments exercise American strategic lift capability and critical support assets for crisis response missions in under-developed areas throughout the world. Finally, they contribute to institution-building in host nations in two ways:

- First, by presenting a positive role model of a legitimate role for military forces in a democratic society;
- Second, to the extent military forces are permitted to interact with host nation agencies on a functional basis, they contribute to the strengthening of those institutions as foundations for democratic development and economic pluralism.

Recalling that stability is not defined as the status quo, but rather as orderly change, it is clear that much good work has been done already to promote the strategic objective of nation development. In short, the foundation has been laid for strategic nation and regional development plans. What remains now is the adoption of the whole notion of the operational continuum and institutionalisation and the role that Military Engineers can play in achieving nation development while simultaneously accomplishing other national military strategy tasks. The combined DoD/non-DoD effort in Latin American nation development is currently making an important contribution. It has considerable number of tools available which can be applied to the task at hand. Not only can these tools be applied to advance the concept of nation development, they can be also positive forces as the national anti-drug effort and the theatre economy of force strategy. There are additional USACE management tools which, if funded and brought to bear on the situation, can greatly increase the effect of limited dollar resources.

Managing Change in Latin America: Further Observations

CRESENCIO S. ARCOS, JR.

For the last 45 years, US relations with Latin America were essentially frozen in the Cold War and its national security implications. During those sporadic moments when the United States turned its attention to Latin America, it sought, mostly with greater and greater amounts of aid, to wage and win the war on its doorstep. Yet with the Soviet Union dissolved into many parts and global communism in hopeless disarray, there is an unprecedented opportunity in the region to promote and manage change.

The end of the Cold War liberates the United States to focus on its true interests in these natural allies as stronger and more democratic neighbours with growing markets. The United States is free to encourage in the region real economic reform, a paring down of swollen civilian and military bureaucracies, the development of functioning and fair judicial systems and the lessening of corruption. Unfettered by fear, the United States and Latin America can work together to fortify the hemisphere while stemming the northward tide of illegal immigration.

Although economic and political realities have ordained that US aid to Latin America decrease, the United States can avoid a commensurate decline in its influence with a reworking of policy aims and methods. To maintain the US position in the region, however, energies (and dollars) should be carefully and coherently focused. The changing parameters of global politics present many challenges for the United States as it constructs a policy for Latin America fashioned to fit the new world.

The Cold War

For nearly half a century, US policy in Latin America reacted to the defining force: Soviet communism. Three seminal events, occurring in Guatemala, Cuba and Nicaragua/El Salvador, helped to shape this policy and indeed, the dialogue that prevailed since World War II. All three events intensified US national security concerns in the region. In each instance, the United States responded with greater amounts of aid and military assistance agreements. Given the often rigid and polarised nature of Cold War dialogue in the United States, many observers on the left and right posed the Latin American conflict as one primarily between forces of evil and good.

In 1954 Guatemala elected a left-wing president, Colonel Jacobo Arbenz Guzman. Arbenz, whose populist rhetoric included agrarian reform proposals, assumed power at a time when intense anti-communism predominated within the United States. The communists and their allies were perceived as unified, determined and globally insidious, and Arbenz raised fears that this quest had made it to the American continent. Although the US-backed coup that deposed Arbenz went virtually unopposed, the United States hastened to fortify Latin America against the perceived communist threat. From 1952 to 1955 Washington signed bilateral military assistance accords with at least 11 Latin American countries.

In 1959 Cuba's takeover by Fidel Castro and the communists led to the Bay of Pigs and the Cuban Missile Urisis. Seeking to contain the encroaching Soviet communist tide, the United States crafted a response for Latin America in the Alliance for Progress. The Kennedy administration's new policy included promises of up to $20 billion in economic aid for Latin America and brought with it millions of dollars in support of increased military supply and training programs.

In the late 1970s and early 1980s, the Marxist Sandinistas wrested Nicaragua from General Anastasio Somoza and the Salvadoran civil war began. In response, the Reagan administration fashioned its version of the containment policy to roll back leftist gains. The Reagan Doctrine created military aid programmes to confront Soviet-Cuban subversion. Even though these programmes had the stated aim of professionalising the region's militaries, they were actually formulated to fortify Latin American countries against the forces of the Left.

These three events – in Guatemala, Cuba and Nicaragua/El Salvador – roused enough furor in the US body politic to spur policy changes designed to strengthen local militaries. Each time, the spectre of threatened US national security was raised, and each time, those tiny countries to the South became tangible arenas in which anti-Yankee sentiment could create superpower conflict – conflict that would subside when the threat perception dissipated. Washington's policy often seemed reactive, militaristic and laden with fear – in short, a wartime policy set in the Cold War.

As in wartime, US goals for Latin America that posed a conflict with the prioritised elements of national security policy were given scant focus or energy. It became convenient for US policy-makers to look the other way so as not to bear witness to the excesses of military strongmen and ruling oligarchs. In responding to the dangers posed by Soviet communism, the United States tended to focus less on human rights, democratic development and strengthening judicial systems. Confronting security threats was the clear priority.

In the effort to bolster small and weak nations against Soviet-Cuban pretensions, the United States inadvertently nurtured some negative aspects of Latin America, including 'caudillismo', 'caciquismo' and a political culture that grants a mystique to 'la bota' or the military. To be sure, the fundamental elements of these countries can be found in their historical, political and cultural roots. Nonetheless, most military and civilian elites of modern Latin American societies gathered strength during the Cold War, to influence some of their countries' strongest political values.

During the Cold War, the policy dialogue about Latin America within the United States rarely progressed beyond a shouting match between liberal and conservative. Although there were sincere people on both sides, for the most part extreme views dominated the discussion. For the conservatives, Latin America conjured up the threat of Marxist-Leninist revolutionaries bent on using violent means to destabilise one valid government after another on their way towards the United States. For the liberals. Latin America consisted of military dictators using torture and death squads to wipe out their opposition while looting the public treasury for their own gain. The polarised nature of these images precluded progress or rational discussion, yet both distorted versions of Latin America were successfully transmitted to the general population.

Legacies of the Cold War

With the end of the Cold War, Central America seems transformed. Observers see constitutional democracies from Mexico to Panama. Everywhere, it seems, elections are fair, political debate is legal, the press free, free markets respected. Civilian leaders look and sound like familiar, safe technocrats. Armed opposition is again the realm of terrorists or criminals. The armed forces appear tamed because their leaders no longer don presidential sashes.

Yet the creation of Central America as a democratic, capitalistic bloc was neither accidental nor unexpected, nor was it the result of a sudden and simultaneous realisation across the region of the benefits of democracy over dictatorships, free markets over planned economies. The United States, with its insistence on democratisation, obviously played an important role in the rise of anti-communist sentiment throughout Central America. Democracy's spread in the region was hardly serendipitous.

Now, free of the Cold War rubric, the United States can turn clear eyes on Central America. Are they really democrats? Do they truly have faith in an egalitarian process of governing and choosing who governs? Are they really capitalists? Have they honestly shed their mercantilist, protectionist ways to become free market converts?

United States policy-makers now have the luxury of unobstructed vision. However, they should be judicious, because the rhetoric of everybody involved – from presidents to businessmen – will provide just what Washington wants to hear. Except for Costa Rica, where democratic roots extend back almost a century, and Belize, with its British tradition, in most of the Central American regimes democracy is still brittle and weak, and each economy is still largely controlled by the state. Rare is the Central American nation where equality is given force of law, legal rights always respected, or decisions based on supply and demand.

Rather, in Central America, the Cold War was 'won' at a cost to its societies. Civilians and militaries alike grew increasingly reliant on international aid. Militaries became ever more independent of civilians accustomed to ceding responsibility to their booted compatriots. Today, civilian corruption in Latin America is rampant, and members of each community, military and civilian, seek impunity from their country's ineffective judicial systems.

It is this search for impunity, more than profit or power *per se*, that often drives these societies. Cloaking him with an aura of imperviousness, impunity gives its bearer a seat above the law. The recent civilianisation of these societies has not discouraged impunity or the desperate search for it, but instead has merely widened its province. In the past, legal systems under military rule exempted the military leadership from the reach of justice, while civilians were generally treated under existing law. Now, civilians increasingly want their share; there is no real justice, just varying shades of impunity. The relevant rule of thumb is: 'a deal for my friend, the law for my enemy.'

Managing Change

The United States is at a crucial crossroads in its relations with Latin America. As in the past, the United States could choose to ignore the region, keeping Latin America on the back pages until another crisis vaults it into the headlines, again forcing a US reaction. The United States could continue formulating Latin America policy and conducting the dialogue under the rubric of national security, giving shorter shrift to other considerations while focusing on perceived threats. The drug war, for example, could fill the threat vacuum left by the end of the Cold War. The challenge posed by the drug war is a familiar one: how to ensure that Latin American partners are not compromised by the vast sums of money involved in the battle.

Or the United States could choose to be serious about Latin America and its economic and political future. Latin America, with its 450 million people, is important to North Americans: geographically, economically, culturally, both are intertwined. Latin American problems, unresolved, will eventually become US problems. America's policies could reflect a new consensus that the best national interests are served when these neighbouring countries have stability, strength and buying power.

The United States faces twin challenges in dealing with Latin America: first, to nudge governments and economic elites towards freer markets, and second, to encourage the growth of stronger democratic institutions. In the economic sector, the United States fosters programmes in Latin America that create conditions for self-sustaining economic growth. Many countries in the region are already starting on this path; they recognise that Mexico and Chile earned steady growth trajectories by working to attract investment rather than foreign aid. The Enterprise for the Americas programme adopted this outlook, bringing economic good sense to bear on policy and thus loosening the stranglehold of debt on the neighbouring countries, supporting their independence from aid, and encouraging moves towards privatisation and adherence to market forces.

To address Latin America's economic challenge, the United States supports well-planned programmes that aim at reducing the size and scope of the central government by selling off inefficient state enterprises, cutting tariffs and trimming bureaucratic red tape. Washington's policies encourage structural adjustment reforms that include reduced external debts, equitable and efficient taxation strategies, reduced regulations, decreased government spending and realistically valued currencies. In the legal arena, the United States has urged that intellectual property laws be implemented and that land title systems be made transparent and fair to enable these countries to attract foreign investment.

Latin America's economic challenge has an environmental component. The Rio 'Earth Summit' of June 1992 underscored the view that governments and citizens must begin to act as the caretakers they are of their environment and natural resources. Routine depletion of resource such as water, fish and forest by overuse and mismanagement and damaging practices such as slash-and-burn agriculture must be curtailed. The Enterprise for the Americas plan included a provision that links debt forgiveness and environmental protection; such policies with an eye towards conservation permit development while working to preserve irreplaceable natural wealth.

Washington's policy for Latin America also supports moves towards strengthening the principles and institutions of democracy. Reforms to improve the technical capabilities and professionalism of the key organs of democratic government are being encouraged. In Honduras and several other Latin American countries, the US government has supported these goals with the Strengthening Democratic Institutions (SDI) programme. The intention of the SDI programme is to foster reforms that depoliticise the business of government by enhancing the technical skills of legislative and court personnel, refashioning operations in court, congress and electoral bodies, and improving the conduct of elections. This kind of programme has become one of the cornerstones of the US post-Cold War approach to Latin America.

Why is SDI so important? In addition to professional, efficient legislative and electoral institutions, a sound judicial system is a fundamental component of a functioning democracy. These societies must confront the matter of impunity before the law, a problem that has mushroomed in recent years. Progress in human rights, in the protection of indigenous groups and in social justice must also be key ingredients of judicial reform.

Nevertheless, despite efforts by the United States, the political will to carry out these reforms must come ultimately from the Latin Americans themselves who are ready to take on the challenges facing their countries.

The Military in Modern Latin America

If there is to be a new age for Latin America, each country's military must participate. Troop levels and equipment stocks in many countries are far larger than are now required by these nations for national security reasons. In some instances a country's military has responded to the diminution of security fears by entering traditionally civilian enterprises such as basic grain production, the manufacture of clothing, cement production and even banking. Yet rather than expanding their mandate in an attempt to justify and preserve their Cold War resource levels, militaries must shrink to fit their decreasing responsibilities.

The message for the future is, I think, clear: inflated military power structures that destabilise the region and drain resources from the people can have no place in the post-Cold War world. The occasional 'Green brigade' engaged in environmental or other tasks is of course a good idea when needed, but large-scale military forays into civilian sectors tend to encourage and exploit the corrupt deal-making and double standards that should be eradicated for these societies to modernise.

The tradition of a paternalistic military could also impede change in these countries, where the military on occasion takes on the guise of a populist 'protector' of the poor from a corrupt political or economic elite. In Latin America, the military assumes some of the power and momentum from the civilians when the latter appear so venal that they squander the public trust.

Civilian governments should take the initiative to begin a rational, democratic debate aimed at matching the size of the militaries to their authentic present and future roles. The United States can contribute to civilianising these societies by supporting institutions such as those that bring civilians and military personnel together for strategic studies, as does the National Defense College in Honduras. Washington policy can continue to support the trend of greater civilian assumption of civic duties. Most importantly, however, the United States can alter the way it conducts relations – exchanging the military-to-military approach for one in which the US government deals with the military primarily through civilian authorities, as has already been done with El Salvador. With the Cold War over, the United states cannot waste the opportunity to experience the supreme luxury of foreign policy: truly flexible objectivity.

Obstacles and Opportunities

Many obstacles obstruct this course. Foremost is the problem of basic Latin American values, habits that roll on well-worn grooves. The traditional, accepted fact of corruption within many Latin American societies could block any sincere desire to change. So many leaders see their tenures primarily as opportunities to enrich themselves and their associates. Pervading all levels and sectors of society in Latin America, corruption transcends politics. Even though corruption affects all nations, its insidious hold on Latin America is the most formidable problem standing in the way of this region's development of a truly democratic, economically strong future.

Another related challenge to a reform-minded US policy for Latin America is the customary method of management in these countries. In the past, the leaders have tended to subvert the promised reforms and problems have arisen when their own misconduct undermined the credibility of any reformist model. The dilemma is clear: can the elites be convinced to play clean, to manage new economic reforms in a free market and to insure the new political reforms that lead to real democracy?

When change is imminent, opposition will rise to meet it. A new structural adjustment policy menaces the status quo in Latin America, a status quo seeded by tradition and culture and wittingly or unwittingly fertilised by the United States. The military, the political parties, the unions, the bureaucracies, even many of the people will so doubt be fiercely protective of their personal rice bowls that seem threatened by any reduction in the power of the state. Most of the Latin American democracies have institutions too weak to be able to withstand too many hits. The newly created columns of democracy are fragile indeed, especially if those who purport to be building them are vulnerable to charges of corruption.

Unconscious tendencies of Latin American society will also act as a counterweight to US goals. In many of these nations, the poor are the first to sacrifice and the last to benefit. If the gap should widen between the top and bottom sectors of Latin American societies, dangerous social upheaval could result. While US policy-makers have had to be alert to these obstacles and combat them when possible, they have also had to do so with fewer resources; political and economic exigencies at home demanded this. To undertake a policy on ground not first softened by a few hundred million dollars is an intimidating concept for the United States and its aid-recipient countries. Yet it can be argued that aid monies are not as useful or necessary today, with our policies based on broader, shared interests. Less assistance certainly offers fewer opportunities for dishonesty at donor community expense in Latin America.

When the US stance is not compromised by arrangements required for its own national security, as was often the case during the Cold War, the United States has a moral force and authority that exceeds its purchasing power. In Honduras in 1991, when the US Embassy spoke out for a just resolution of a case in which military officials stood accused of rape and murder, it was not Uncle Sam's aid money that made the public rally in support with marches and protests. Under the rubric of this policy stance, the United States can regain some of its old shine as an emblem of democracy. Such a shine can replace currency in the foreign policy arena.

Change has already started in many Latin American countries, but it cannot stop. American liberals and conservatives now have the opportunity to see Latin American issues as more than litmus tests for 'patriotism' or 'political correctness', and Latin Americans as more than right-wing thugs, leftist terrorists or drug dealers. Latin America is bound to the United States. Observers on all sides of the political spectrum can now talk to each other rationally and with room for exchange, formulating a policy consensus to direct actions in this area.

Ultimately, it will be members of these Latin American societies themselves who will determine the success of a partnership with the United States based on economic and political reforms. If they respond to encouragement for reforms, the United States can offer much in the way of market access, practical advice, leadership and limited amounts of aid. If they do not, they risk a future which ensures the inefficiency and corruption of the status quo. The challenge is upon us; together we face a rare moment in Latin American history, a juncture that has delivered up an unprecedented opportunity to manage change.

Latin America: The Unfinished Business of Security

DONALD E. SCHULZ
and GABRIEL MARCELLA

Summary of Panel Discussion

The panel discussed three basic questions: (1) How can a democratic government most effectively combat insurgency? (2) What specific lessons can be drawn from the history of insurgencies and, in particular, from the cases of Guatemala and Peru? and (3) How effective are US supply-side efforts to combat drug trafficking?

There was general agreement that democratisation was a key not only to the defeat of insurgencies, but to the creation of conditions that would prevent their re-emergence. The objective of a democratic internal defence is to incorporate as many groups and individuals as possible into the defence process while at the same time bringing them into the democratic process. This means carrying out a democratic revolution at the grassroots level. People must be brought into the system so they will have a stake in its survival.

Institution-building is of crucial importance. Institutions provide the vital linkage through which citizens are brought into the political process and government is made more responsive to their needs and desires. A second key is *legitimacy* and the *rule of law*: A democracy cannot use counter-insurgency methods that undermine its own legitimacy or it risks self-destruction.

Third, there must be *civilian leadership*. Here the British model of counter-insurgency has much to recommend it, emphasising as it does such factors as a comprehensive plan under civilian direction, the predominance of political over military considerations, the importance of using local resources, the need to act in accordance with the role of law and to punish human rights abuses, and the government's contractual obligation with its citizens. The point is that legitimacy is a weapon, and either you use it against the enemy or he will use it against you.

Within this general context, several lessons were drawn from the Guatemalan and Peruvian cases. Caesar Sereseres (Professor of Political Science and Dean, University of California, Irvine) noted that, in the former, elections had become part of the military's strategy to win the war; they legitimised the war effort. And the strategy worked. Unfortunately, democratisation remained incomplete. The burden of fighting the insurgency remained disproportionately on the military. Guatemalan civilians tended to withdraw, leaving the army to do the job alone. Moreover, the civilians did not take advantage of the opportunities they had fundamentally to change the judicial process. Consequently, human rights abuses continued. At the same time, corruption (by both military and civilians, but especially the latter) further undercut democracy. And the unwillingness of the United States to hold civilians accountable, as it had done to the military, meant that opportunities to deepen democratisation were largely wasted. That in turn raises the possibility that those gains that have been achieved may be reversed and that the insurgency may at some point regain momentum.

David Scott Palmer (Director, Latin American Studies Program, Boston University) observed that in Peru the situation was even more tenuous. There the restoration of democracy had coincided with a major escalation of human rights abuses. Elections and civilian governments coexisted with military dictatorship in the form of regional war zones. As the state proved itself incapable of dealing with the country's profound socio-economic crisis, moreover, ordinary citizens increasingly began to take on the responsibility for their own survival. The consequence was a growing informalisation of Peruvian society, economy, and polity. Meanwhile, the insurgency spread, as the countryside surrounded the cities in classic Maoist fashion.

The culmination of this process of informalisation was the Fujimori presidency. Alberto Fujimori was elected, in large part, because he was perceived to be the personification of anti-politics – of 'politics as usual' – and he has been just that. In implementing the politics of anti-politics, he has sought to undermine the Peruvian Congress, the political parties, and even the military. In effect, he has viewed the armed forces as just one more institution that needs to be put in its place. Palmer suggested that this was a dangerous game and could well come back to haunt him in the form of a military coup or a victory by the only well-institutionalised alternative force, *Sendero Luminoso*. [*Editor's Note*: Since the capture of Abimael Guzman in September 1992, the *Sendero Luminoso* insurgency has experienced serious setbacks from the Fujimori government. Whether these setbacks are decisive remains to be seen.]

Sereseres made some observations about the changing roles and missions of the armed forces in a democratic society. Beyond the obvious need to support democracy, he said that the military would have to assume a more limited national security role and that it would have to share that responsibility with civilians. The military cannot close out a civilian presence within the armed forces. Instead, there needs to be more bridge-building. A civilian-military dialogue must be developed, so that military officers can come to view themselves as the defenders, rather than the victims, of democracy. At the same time, new socio-economic missions have to be developed. (He pointedly noted, however, that the military could not be the police force.) For its part, the United States should support military modernisation and professionalisation. This means more support for military education, but with less emphasis on purely military skills and more on technical and sociological knowledge shaped to the new missions of the military.

The most controversial presentation of the conference was delivered by Kenneth Sharpe, who spoke on 'The Drug War and Democracy in Latin America: What Would Clausewitz Tell Us?'. Sharpe argued that, while the drug trade is a threat to Latin American democracies, so is the drug war. He noted that some of Washington's allies are undemocratic and engage in human rights abuses, and he questioned the wisdom of strengthening these elements by giving them US aid. Moreover, he observed that, while the drug trade is a threat to democracy, it also sustains economies that would otherwise be in such crisis as to threaten political stability and democracy.

Ambassador Edwin G. Corr (formerly US Ambassador to Bolivia, Peru and EL Slavador) closed the discussion by agreeing that the primary thrust of the drug war should be domestic. However he noted that the necessary amount of money has never been spent and that what was spent has been largely on the domestic side. He also strongly endorsed Caesar Sereseres' comments about the importance of civilian responsibility. He said that, if the civilians do not exercise the responsibility to create institutions and take on the tasks and functions that the military surrenders, then there will be a real problem. If the civilians do not transform their societies, the insurgencies will return. Within this context, he stressed the importance of developing a civilian-military dialogue and argued that the adoption of new military missions would not necessarily undermine Latin American democracies.

Reflecting the policy of the outgoing Bush administration as well as his own views, Bernard Aronson, Assistant Secretary of State, addressed the broad issue of the role of the Latin American miliary in a democracy and the role of US policy. In our time, he stated, we have witnessed the competition of the ideas of democracy and totalitarianism. Democracy triumphed. The current worldwide democratic revolution began in Latin America during the 1970s.

Aronson said that Latin America faces any number of threats to democracy, most notably drugs, debt, economic underdevelopment, corruption, and a crisis of participation. If these challenges are not met effectively, democracy will be at risk. In addressing these threats in view of the New World Order, the Latin American nations and their armed forces need to redefine the roles and missions of the military. If the issue is not properly addressed, he argued, many Latin American militaries may revert to the role of arbiter of internal threats.

To preclude reverting to an internal threat orientation, the armed forces need to undertake legitimate missions as part of international peacekeeping forces. This argues for a revitalised Organization of American States, something that has been taking place. In addition, Aronson counselled that the gap between Latin American civilian and military leaders be narrowed – the view of the military as somehow apart from civil society must disappear. A dialogue encompassing military and civilian ideas needs to take place. He recommended that the United States rethink its international military education programs to promote such dialogue.

Major General John Ellerson introduced the panel by noting that the title recognised the fact that we are entering a new era and face new challenges. Things that were unthinkable a few years ago are now possible. Yet, there are also enduring realities that need to be dealt with. There is still much to be done. Low intensity conflict is often not very low in intensity, and peacetime engagement is often not very peaceful. The challenge for this panel is to chart a course into the new world, recognising that this is not a blank sheet of paper and that there are still many rocks out there that need to be avoided.

Caesar Sereseres on Guatemala

The first presentation was by Caesar Sereseres on 'Guatemala: Lessons Learned for Democracy in Low Intensity Conflict'.

Sereseres noted that there were a lot of analytical dangers in drawing general conclusions from a single, very narrow case study but said that Guatemala provides a lot of insight as to how a society and a (military) institution deal with an internal war and also how the United States deals with such a situation. There are two core questions: one has to do with the role of the military in a democratic society that is engaged in an internal war, and the other involves US policy (especially military-to-military relationships) in working in a positive way with Latin American military institutions. How do the experiences of Guatemala help us address these two issues?

With regard to the role of the military in a democratic society, he made several points:

First, regardless of its ideology and corporate character, the military, especially in the 1990s, is essentially a national institution that exists to support and defend a political process, including certain values and institutional arrangements. Democracy is an essential feature of international relations, particularly in American foreign policy.

Second, although its role is national security, in the 1990s the military will have to assume a much more limited responsibility and, most important, will have to share that responsibility. In the past, the military has assumed that it was to its benefit to monopolise the responsibility for security issues. He argues that, regardless of the country and the institution, it has now become fully recognised that it is an enormous psychological, political and professional burden to assume complete and total responsibility for national security. That must now be shared with civilians and civilian institutions.

Third, the military will have to assume responsibility for the high-risk micro-socio-economic projects that establish services and authority in areas that the central government and national bureaucracies tend not to go.

Fourth, in its contact with the general population (through both its officers and enlisted men), the miliary is in effect a socialisation agent to foster and develop a civic culture.

Fifth, a new responsibility that has yet to be defined by individual militaries is that of engaging in regional and global responsibilities/co-operation.

Sixth, the military cannot be the police force of the nation.

Finally, it cannot close out a civilian presence within the military institution or within the society at large.

As for US policy, Sereseres said that there were three essential lessons to be drawn from past experience. These are essentially ways in which the United States needs to think about the future of the Latin American militaries within a democratic setting; they should serve as the pillars of US policy:

First and foremost, there has to be support for military modernisation, including educational skills and the professional military knowledge needed to be productive in the twenty-first century. There will be less emphasis on purely military skills and more stress on technical and socio-economic forms of knowledge shaped to the mission of the military.

Second, the United States must serve as a catalyst for bridge-building between the civilians and the military. With some exceptions, there has been little change between these two cultures. Their psychologies are distinct; their educational systems are distinct; the ways in which they look at each other are distinct; and despite the fact that several military institutions have almost driven themselves into the ground in self-destruction, most have not learned the lessons of the past. And neither have the civilians.

Third, US policy must facilitate communications and cooperation between hemispheric military institutions.

Sereseres went on to give a bit of historical background on the situation in Guatemala. He noted that between 1944 and 1954, there had been a 'social revolution' in Guatemala. The first elected civilian president, Juan José Arévalo, instituted major reforms in Guatemalan society. Since his departure in 1951, there have been approximately 42 years of governance. Ten of the 13 chiefs of state have been military officers. Eleven of the 42 years have been under elected civilian presidents; 8 years have been under military government; 23 years have been spent under elected military officers. In these 42 years there have been five successful coups. The country has gone through over 30 years of internal war, beginning in 1962 in the aftermath of the military reformist coup of November 1960. During this three-decade period, we have seen two generations of guerrillas, fighting different strategies and pursuing two different social revolutions. At least 60,000 lives have been lost. There have been over 600,000 refugees and displaced persons and a standing army that has grown from less than 12,000 in the early 1960s to well over 40,000 today.

What lessons can be learned from this experience? First, the military has remained the central national institution of Guatemala, for better as well as for worse. There exists a military culture that has been influenced not only by the war but by the society that it serves. And added to that has been the nature of American foreign policy. To put it mildly, US policy has not been very consistent. There have been a lot of zigzags and U-turns to the point where Guatemalans could describe US policy as schizophrenic and the United States could describe Guatemalan behaviour as paranoid. And there is a little bit of truth in both characterisations. Not only are the Guatemalan generals and colonels of today the products of the war, but they have seen US policy change every four to six years with or without any good explanations.

In summarising, in terms of lessons learned, he said that five points can be made about the Guatemalan case: First, there is an unequal burden in fighting the insurgency. Whether it is a military or a civilian government, ultimately the burden is absorbed by the military institution. The civilians quite often tend to withdraw or disengage in dealing with the insurgency, politically, socially, and economically, leaving the military to do the job alone. That causes all kinds of unintended problems.

Second, the civilians, partially as a response to the military but largely as a civilian problem, have not taken advantage of the opportunities presented by the systemic crisis to, for instance, drastically and radically change the judicial process. This only encourages paramilitary and death squad strategies. In a country where there is no confidence in the judicial process, the penal system, etc., time and time again, opportunities to change the system have been wasted.

Third, elections became part of the military's strategy to legitimise the war against the insurgents. It was a strategy that was enunciated after the March 1982 coup. It was carried out in less than four years; *and it worked*. The problem is that the elections by themselves did not bring about the necessary change; they simply changed the political context of the war. Remarkably, this was sufficient to effect a political and military offensive against the guerrillas that was successful in 1985.

Fourth, there is the unpleasant interface between democracy and corruption. This has been the Achilles' heel of US policy, and it has been the Achilles' heel of the democratic process in Guatemala and many other countries. The military is part of the problem; but by far the civilians have been the leaders in the area of corruption and inefficiency. They themselves do not institute a system of accountability. They can accuse the military of having no accountability procedures in terms of money, personnel and operations, but the civilians themselves have made no effort to make these changes.

Finally, the last lesson concerns the US unwillingness and inability to hold the fire to the feet of Guatemalan civilians as closely and constantly as it has held it to the feet of the military. We have trouble imposing the same kind of standards on civilians that we impose on the military. He suggested that Guatemala over the past 30 years has been a clear indication as to how the US has dealt with countries and institutions at war.

This is a dangerous mix because Guatemala, as well as Venezuela and other countries, can easily step backward. He said that unless these bridges are built and unless the military is willing to accept a civilian presence and unless the civilians are willing to accept a critical role for the military in national policy, democracy would not work. It would be but a passing phase.

In closing, he quoted a statement from Luigi Einaudi which he said hit at the heart of the dilemma that US policy faced in dealing with the military as professional organisations: 'We have seldom had the luxury of dealing with the Latin American military outside the optic of American domestic politics – as human rights, as democracy or as proliferation.' Einaudi pins it down to the very crux. The future consolidation of democracy in the Western Hemisphere requires true civil-military co-operation. To keep those civilian governments requires that the civilians develop a dialogue with the military so that the military can see themselves as the defenders, rather than the victims, of democracy.

Gustavo Gorriti on Peru

At this point, the Peruvian freelance journalist Gustavo Gorriti arrived. Since he could only stay for a short time, he was allowed to speak on his topic: 'Counter-insurgency Doctrine and the Relationship with Democracy.'

Gorriti began by explaining why he had become interested in the subject. He noted that he had begun working as a journalist at a time when the Shining Path insurgency was just beginning. This was also a time in which democracy was being restored in Peru. It was a time of high hopes and yet it also coincided with the rise of this strange, difficult-to-understand insurgency. He recalled one of his early interviews with the first minister of the interior in the Belaunde government. The minister had told him that, in spite of all the pressure he was under to react with repression, he would not 'order good pyjamas and dynamite suppositories for captured Shining Path militants'. Gorriti came away from the interview instinctively persuaded that he had the right approach.

Yet the problem was that although the minister and the Belaunde government knew what should not be done, they did not know what had to be done. Within a few years, military officers and other officials were telling Gorriti that this was a war, and certain costs has to be assumed. The only way to extract tactical intelligence was through torture. Thus, within a few years of the inauguration of democracy, Peru's human rights record was worse than those of the most notorious Latin American dictatorships. In 1989, for instance, for the third year in a row, Peru had one of the worst human rights records in the world.

In Ayacucho Department, from 1982 to 1988, more than 6,000 people were killed or disappeared. That is twice the number Pinochet's government (in Chile) killed or who had disappear in 16 years. One must keep in mind also that the population of Ayacucho is only slightly more than half a million people. What happened in Peru was that the zones placed under emergency, which were those most affected by internal war, became for all practical purposes an area under military government and a *de facto* dictatorship within the larger democratic framework. And so you had the corrosive growth of military government inside democracy. At the same time, the insurgency spread, following the classic people's war pattern, with the cities encircled by the countryside. For years, Peru has lived a kind of political schizophrenia not unknown in many Latin American countries, only more acute. This process of systemic weakening culminated in the April 1992 coup, which ended the 12-year experiment in Peruvian democracy.

In terms of its broader significance, the Peruvian case showed (and this is confirmed by over 30 years of studies on internal wars in Latin America) that (1) democracies are not immune to insurgencies; (2) insurgencies do not directly overthrow democratic regimes (there are no historical examples of such overthrows); and (3) the way a democratic government controls an insurgency may not necessarily be critical for the war's outcome, but it is certainly critical for its own survival. It is just this lesson that is so often overlooked by officials: A democracy cannot use counter-insurgency methods that are not built on democratic legitimacy.

Gorriti asked how democratic regimes can control their insurgencies without defeating themselves in the process. He referred to the three most important counter-insurgency doctrines: the French, the British, and the American. All of these, he noted, were forged in colonial circumstances. He said that the British approach is best suited because it is largely predicated on a low profile and an economy of force; on trying to find solutions that would not require great investments in manpower or equipment; on using to their utmost local resources; and building close co-operation with civilian authority. To these, Sir Robert Thompson's theoretical contributions add: the necessity of having a comprehensive plan under civilian direction; the need for government to act in accordance with the law; the need to use legitimacy as a weapon and as a fulfillment of the government's contractual obligations with its people; to treat torture and extrajudicial execution as crimes; and consider popular support not as an exercise in behaviour modification to be attained by scientific techniques, but as a primary exercise of free will.

Gorriti stressed that a democratic internal defence relies on the principles of (1) civilian control; and (2) the predominance of the political over the military. He said that the most important lesson that can be drawn from historical examples concerns the tremendous need for civilian leadership. The two most important examples of such leadership are the Philippines under Ramón Magsaysay and Venezuela under Betancourt. Several policies that these strong leaders put into effect were considered counter-productive by some of the experts of the day. In Venezuela, for instance, some experts felt that restrictions imposed by the government on the internal security forces made it very difficult to mount an effective counter-insurgency effort. But Betancourt knew better. By using legitimacy and the rule of law (including using the war as a means of establishing the rule of law) and by granting generous amnesties (which were offered by his successors as well), they were able to defeat the insurgency and get through with an exemplary (until 1992) democratic model which in its time was considered the most threatening one not only by the Castroite revolutionaries but also by the Dominican dictator Rafael Trujillo.

In practical terms, what the examples of Betancourt and Magsaysay mean is that, for a democracy to survive in a state of internal war, it will have to fight as a democracy but readjust its mechanisms to cope with the demands of internal war. A besieged democracy fighting for its life cannot function as it would in peacetime. It must limit secondary freedoms in order to save essential liberties. It has simplified political measures related to internal war efforts in order to make them practical and effective so as to parallel the legal systems of enforcement that enable the society to cope with emergencies. In the final analysis, the objective of any democratic internal defence is precisely that society, throughout the emergency period, incorporate into the process as many groups and individuals as possible and also incorporate them dramatically into the democratic process so they will have a stake in keeping it alive and robust. This means to carry out the democratic revolution at the grassroots level, to energise the country and the people to lead the internal war effort, which is, in short, a defence of democratic legitimacy. In the end, the best way for a fragile democracy to defend itself is to carry out a democratic revolution while going about the business of trying to win the war.

David Scott Palmer on Peru

The third speaker was David Scott Palmer, who spoke on the topic of 'Democracy Fights Internal War: The Requirements for Winning in Peru.' Palmer suggested that institution-building was at the heart of the 'lingering challenges to security'. He noted that according to social science theory, the more institutionalised a polity, society or economy – namely, the more autonomous its institutions and the better able they are to pursue their own interests – the more 'developed' it is. One reason why so many observers are so enthusiastic about what has been happening in Latin America during these last 10 to 15 years is that it appears that we are witnessing a process of redemocratisation, in which we are seeing the development and routinisation of democratic procedures. We are not talking here about complete or fully consolidated democracy. Rather, we are talking about the routinisation of the procedures and practices associated with the process of getting citizens plugged into the centre and getting the centre to be responsive to the citizens. That is what democracy is all about. Between 1930 and 1965, just about 50 per cent of all changes of government in Latin America occurred through nonconstitutional means. But if you look at the 1980s, you find that less than 20 per cent of government changes were through nonconstitutional means. And furthermore, in two-thirds of the changes that occurred through constitutional means in the 1980s – a decade in which there were fewer coups than in any other decade since independence – there were victories by opposition parties. What we are witnessing in Latin America is a process of substitution of an electoral opposition for the military in the latter's historic role as an institution of last resort – an institution to turn to when the political system became immobilised or unable to deal with the various problems that faced the broader society.

Palmer said that Peru is a fascinating case for various reasons. For one thing, this is a country that has in combination one of the worst sets of problems of any country in the hemisphere – including insurgency, drug trafficking, a terrible economic crisis, and a social situation in which two-thirds of all Peruvians live below the poverty line. What we have been witnessing over the past 25 years has been a process of informalisation that has been taking place in the society, the economy and, most recently, the political process. He hypothesised that, in at least some respects, as the government became less able in the late 1970s and early 1980s to deal with social problems, society itself began to take on real responsibility for dealing with those problems. There was a proliferation of grassroots organisations that were designed to deal with a host of issues, some of which were politically inspired but many of which were not. Many of these responses were simply local adaptations to local needs and problems in the absence of an effective government presence *or* in the presence of a government which could not do the job right. (As many would argue, it was the military government's fate to try to transform Peru at the grassroots, even as it lacked the resources to be able to do that effectively.) Moreover, in the 1980s, as the economy worsened, there was an effort on the part of Peruvians to gain employment and other opportunities to survive. As individuals, families and other collectivities, they began to work out their own solutions, and we began to see, beginning in the 1970s and expanding dramatically in the early 1980s, a very large informal economic sector. As Hernando de Soto has noted, at least 40 per cent of the Peruvian economy is based on informal activities that never make their way into national economic data.

What is fascinating, he said, is that even as democracy returned to Peru in 1980 and even as we have seen three successive democratic elections, in spite of all the problems associated with other aspects of society – 25,000 people killed in the terror and insurgency, inflation of over 2 million per cent cumulatively between 1985 and 1990, real wages declining by 70 per cent in the 1980s, government salaries reduced by 80 to 90 per cent even as government employment increased by 400,000 – there is still large-scale, overwhelming support for the democratic process, as imperfect as it has been. This includes two successive elected governments, both of which in different ways were unable or unwilling to respond effectively to the needs of the population. And it leads to the election of 1990 where there was ushered in another figure – an opposition figure – who represented in his person the antithesis of 'politics as usual'. He is the epitome in civilian guise of the erstwhile 'politics of anti-politics' of the military governments of the 1960s and 1970s. He represented the antithesis of politics as usual – and has proceeded as President to do exactly that.

Fujimori is in the process, consciously or unconsciously, with substantial popular support, of implementing the informality of politics in Peru. Undermining the parties (working around them), the *autogolpe* (self-coup) of April 1992 was designed to wrench control from a Congress that looked like it was going to spend the last half of Fujimori's term destroying him and whatever he was trying to do. At least, it would have made life very difficult for him. And this could have been done, since opposition parties controlled the majority of seats in Congress. In the elections of 22 November 1992 a large portion of the population either did not vote or spoiled their ballots. Fujimori set it up in such a way that with 38 per cent of the vote his forces were able to get a majority in the constitutional convention which will adopt the constitution and then will become the Congress. The groups that participated, with only two exceptions, are groups which are not traditional parties of Peru. The traditional parties of Peru did not participate. This is the informalisation of politics. It carries over into a relationship between President Fujimori and the military institution. Through his politics of anti-politics approach, he has also treated the military institution as one more organisation that needs to be put in its place.

Palmer said that the way that Fujimori has gone about this led to the failed coup of Friday, 13 November 1992. The leader of that coup was concerned that Fujimori was slowly undermining the professional capacity of the armed forces and their 30-year struggle to build a very professionalised military in which professional advancement is based on merit, rather than one's political views or loyalty to a particular civilian or political party. It is a judgment of a variety of people in Peru, as of early December 1992, that this is a very dangerous game. That in the final analysis the informalisation of the society, the economy, and now the polity could very well come back to haunt Fujimori through either a successful coup or (equally likely) a well-institutionalised alternative force – namely Shining Path (*Sendero Luminoso*). As much as they have been adversely affected by the recent capture of scores of key people, the fateful 12 September 1992 capture of Abimael Guzman and 20 of his associates, Shining Path is now in the process of reorganising. It is going back into the countryside, reforming, reorganising, and reidentifying itself before going on to the next stage.

Palmer said that we must remember that Shining Path spent 17 years in various modalities preparing for the armed struggle. This is not an overnight guerrilla movement. The organisation, even though it now lacks its founder and long-time leader, is still a potent, organised force. Within the context of the informalisation of other sectors of Peruvian society, it may be the most potent force outside the military establishment at this particular juncture. The question is: how will the Shining Path reorganise and reset its priorities and agenda for the future? This could take several forms.

Two key questions are: (1) How well will the military respond to the challenge? and, (2) How effectively will the government implement its economic program to the grassroots? For the moment, Peru is basking in the euphoria of Guzmán's capture. This was a major blow to *Sendero*, but a far cry from its total defeat.

The first discussant was Max G. Manwaring, who observed that old Karl (Clausewitz) must be rolling in his grave.

Manwaring said that there is a view (or formula) that states that democracy equals elected civilian government and dictatorship equals military rule; therefore, if you get rid of the military, you *ipso facto* have democracy. He noted that there is a corollary to this also – namely, that the military has no legitimate role: there is no external threat and the internal threat takes us back to military dictatorship. Therefore, we cannot talk to the military or use them to do anything. You have to go around them. Yet in so doing, you miss a major opportunity to influence those political, economic, and social systems you want to influence because, like it or not, Latin American military institutions are a reality and must be dealt with.

Manwaring observed that there is a forgotten dimension of the drug war that goes beyond the military. There is more than one centre of gravity. Another centre is legitimacy; a third is demand. To ignore the latter as being too difficult to deal with is absurd.

The second discussant was Ambassador Edwin E. Corr. Ambassador Corr suggested that Caesar Sereseres had made several extremely important points. Placing responsibility on civilians as well as the military is crucial. If the civilians do not exercise their responsibility to create institutions and pick up the tasks and functions that the military surrenders, you will have a real problem. Civilians have to do their part. He said that he is convinced of the necessity of civilians transforming their societies. That is the key. If they do not it, the insurgency will just come back. We cannot do it for them, but we can help. He noted the importance of establishing a civil-military dialogue.

With regard to the drug war, he agreed with Ken Sharpe that the main thrust must be in the United States, dealing with demand. But he noted that we have never spent the amount of money that was necessary and that what we have spent has been largely on the domestic side. Of the $12 billion spent on narcotics control, never more than 5 per cent has gone to the overseas programme.

He also believes that the Andean countries are hurt more by the cocaine trade than they are helped. The trade may be an economic plus in the short run. But how do you measure the cost of the total corruption of your police, judicial, and other systems?

He went on to note that the military in every country has roles that go beyond the use of force. In the United States, for instance, the Army Corps of Engineers has done a lot in terms of roadbuilding, bridgebuilding, etc. The Army played a major role in the settlement of the West. If Latin Americans want to use their militaries the same way, that does not *necessarily* mean that this will undermine democracy.

Conclusion: An Agenda for US Policy-makers

The 'Warriors in Peacetime' conference reached a new level of sophisticated dialogue between civilians and military officials in this Hemisphere. The conference was designed to produce new insights on what military institutions ought to do in the post-Cold War era as well as what their roles ought to be in democracy. The discussion of 'The Unfinished Business of Security' reminds us that the New World Order has by no means eliminated the need for armed forces. At the same time, the opportunity is at hand to redefine US policy towards the Latin American militaries.

Such a redefinition is a unique challenge at a time when the United States is itself redefining its global military strategy and reducing the size of its armed forces. The Latin American experience debated throughout the conference recommends that civilians and military work together closely to define their responsibilities in matters of national defence. Both the Peruvian and Guatemalan cases speak eloquently of the need for effective civilian leadership of counter-insurgency operations. We will go further: civilian leaders must develop the professional capacity to exercise prudent, effective, and confident control of the military instrument. The major challenge ahead in Latin American countries (and in some the challenge is greater) is to develop such levels of civil-military cooperation in order to deepen the democratic systems now emerging. Democracy is not possible without civilian control. Absent civilian control, military professionalism is not possible.

What of the role of US policy? In a time when the United States is redefining its global role and focusing on strengthening the domestic power base, there is a serious danger that the above agenda will be relegated to secondary or tertiary priority in US policy. The frankness and intensity of the exchanges of views between military officers and civilians during the conference indicate that such a prospect would be a serious setback to the democratisation theme in US policy for Latin America. We need to sustain our progress through a policy of constructive engagement with the Latin American civilians and military. Such engagement would stress the primacy of civilian leadership in national defence and the complementarity of a doctrine of democratic military professionalism. The United States, with its vast experience and wisdom in civilian control of military professionals, can be the catalyst for making this happen. The interaction for such policy would take place at three levels: (1) empowerment of civilian officials and academics in military affairs via education in mechanisms and norms of civilian control, in defence budgeting, intelligence, strategy, logistics, laws of armed combat, and new missions, such as peacekeeping; (2) civilian-military relations in the conduct of diplomacy and in crisis decision-making; and (3) civilian control of the conduct of military operations through the various intensities of war – low, mid, and high.

Appendix: Latin American Defence Data

TABLE 1
DEFENCE EXPENDITURES IN LATIN AMERICA
PERCENTAGES OF GDP/GNP

	1985	1989	1990
Argentina	2.9	1.2	1.2
Bolivia	2.0	3.7	--
Brazil	0.8	0.4	0.2
Chile	7.8	2.4	2.0
Colombia	0.8	0.9	2.3
Costa Rica	0.7	1.1	1.1
Cuba	9.6	5.1	--
Dominican Republic	1.1	0.9	--
Ecuador	1.8	2.2	2.3
El Salvador	4.4	3.5	2.8
Guatemala	1.8	--	0.9
Haiti	1.5	0.8	--
Honduras	2.1	--	2.1
Mexico	0.7	0.3	0.3
Nicaragua	--	--	--
Panama	2.0	--	--
Paraguay	1.3	1.4	--
Peru	4.5	3.9	3.7
Uruguay	2.5	--	--
Venezuela	1.3	0.9	1.1

Source: The International Institute for Strategic Studies, *The Military Balance, 1991–1992* (London: Brassey's, 1991), p.215.

TABLE 2
SIZE OF LATIN AMERICAN ARMED FORCES, 1990–91

	ARMY	NAVY	AIR FORCE	COAST GUARD	POLICE
Argen-tina	45,000	25,000	13,000	13,000	15,000
Bolivia	23,000	4,000	4,000	--	13,850
Brazil	196,000	50,000	50,700	--	243,000
Chile	54,000	25,000	12,800	1,600	27,000
Colombia	115,000	12,000	7,000	1,500	80,000
Costa Rica	--	--	--	--	7,500
Cuba	145,000	13,500	22,000	--	19,000
Dominican Republic	15,000	4,000	4,200	--	15,000
Ecuador	50,000	4,800	3,000	200	--
El Sal-vador	40,000	1,200	2,400	--	12,000
Guate-mala	37,000	1,200	1,400	--	10,100
Haiti	7,400	--	150	250	--
Honduras	14,400	1,000	2,100	--	5,000
Mexico	130,000	37,000	8,000	--	--
Nicara-gua	27,000	1,500	2,000	--	11,650
Panama	--	--	--	--	--
Paraguay	12,500	3,500	1,000	--	8,000
Peru	72,000	18,000	15,000	600	70,000
Uruguay	16,000	3,500	3,400	2,000	1,150
Venezu-ela	34,000	11,000	7,000	--	23,000 National Guard

Source: The International Institute for Strategic Studies, *The Military Balance, 1991–1992* (London: Brassey's, 1991), pp.185–208.

TABLE 3
COMPARATIVE DEFENCE EXPENDITURES
PERCENTAGES OF GDP/GNP

	1985	1989	1990
United States	6.5	5.6	5.4
Canada	2.2	1.7	1.7
Spain	2.4	1.8	1.8
Soviet Union	--	14.2	11.1
Nigeria	1.3	0.9	1.0
Malaysia	5.6	3.7	3.8
India	3.0	3.3	3.2
Egypt	8.5	7.3	5.6

Source: The International Institute for Strategic Studies, *The Military Balance, 1991–1992* (London: Brassey's, 1991), pp.212–14.

TABLE 4
COMPARATIVE MILITARY PAY IN THOUSANDS OF
US DOLLARS PER MONTH

RANK	BRAZIL	U. S.	U. K.	ITALY	MEXICO
Division General	1.5	8.9	9.4	5	2.3
Brigadier General	1.4	8.8	8.6	4.4	2.0
Colonel	1.2	6	6.7	3.3	1.8
Lieutenant Colonel	1.1	5	5.8	2.5	1.6
Captain	0.8	3.7	3.3	1.3	1.2

Source: 'The Uproar Over Soldiers' Pay', *ISTOE SENHOR* 22 April 1992, in *Foreign Broadcast Information Service, Latin America*, 3 June 1992, p.32.

Notes on Contributors

Gabriel Marcella is Professor of Third World Studies at the US Army War College. From 1987 to 1989 he served as International Affairs Advisor to the Commander-in-Chief of the United States Southern Command, Quarry Heights, Panama.

Juan Rial is a Researcher at the Peitho Sociedad de Análisis Político and a Consultant of Perelli, Rial & Asoc, Montevideo, Uruguay.

Kenneth E. Sharpe is Professor of Political Science at Swarthmore College, Pennsylvania. He has conducted extensive field work in Central America, the Dominican Republic, and Mexico. He is the author of *Peasant Politics: Struggle in a Dominican Village* (John Hopkins UP, 1976) and co-editor with Morris Blachman and William LeoGrande, of *Confronting Revolution: Security Through Diplomacy in Central America* (Pantheon, 1986).

Richard L. Millett is at Southern Illinois University, Edwardsville.

Howard J. Wiarda is Professor of National Security at the National Defense University, Washington, DC. He is also Professor of Political Science at the University of Massachusetts and Visiting Scholar at the Center for Strategic and International Studies (CSIS) in Washington, DC.

Jack A. LeCuyer is a serving US Army Colonel of Engineers and Chief, Army Initiatives Group, a staff element supporting the Army Chiefs of Staff. Colonel LeCuyer graduated from West Point in 1966 and served as an engineer company commander with 1st Air Cavalry Division in Vietnam. He has also served with distinction in Panama, California, Louisiana, Germany and SHAPE (Assistant Executive to SACEUR). He is a graduate of the US Army Command and General Staff College and holds civilian degrees from the John F. Kennedy School of Government, Harvard University, and from the Universita 'degli Studi di Firenze, Italy.

Cresencio Arcos, Jr. is the Principal Deputy Assistant Secretary of State for International Narcotics Matters. A career Foreign Service Officer, he was US Ambassador to Honduras from December 1989 to July 1993. Upon his return, he served on the US Department of State's North American Free Trade Agreement (NAFTA) Task Force. Mr